# perfectly weak

## Casey Graves

Published by Hear My Heart Publishing

ISBN: 978-0-9862331-6-6

A product of the United States of America.
Edited by Joe Hilley and Michelle Lehman
Cover design by Chance Calvert and Victoria Ross

*"Weakness isn't something any of us like to admit. Through her vulnerability, my brave friend Casey shares the freedom and healing that comes when we exchange our weakness for God's strength. As you read this book I pray that you too will experience the beauty in being Perfectly Weak."*

Kim Masengale Lead Pastor's Wife at The Summit Church and Pastor of Summit Women

# Dedication

I am so thankful to Jesus who knows me better than I know myself. He plans ahead for my weaknesses and makes my path straight. He comforts me when I am afraid and empowers me to go ahead anyway. His Word and His presence truly are life to me.

To Justin—
You are a gift to me. For real. You continually push me outside of my safe little box that I try to hide in, and push me to take the adventure. Every single day. You are an extraordinary person that brings so much joy to the girls and me. I have never seen so much energy, joy, passion and leadership bottled up in one person until I met you. You are the reason I can dream. Thank you for believing in me.

To my girls, Charli and Chloe—
You are two very strong, take-on-the-world girls. You challenge me to be better so that I can keep up with you two. I am so thankful God made me to be your mom. I am constantly amazed as I get to watch you both grow into amazing young women of God being influencers for His Kingdom. I can't wait to see what God does in your lives.

Beth Wilson—
Thank you for following the leading of the Holy Spirit to launch into Hear My Heart Publishing to give people like me an opportunity to share their stories. Thank you for taking a chance on me.

Joe Hilley—
Thank you to Joe, whom I still do not know well, for taking a year (or so) of your life to donate your expertise, time and energy toward making this book better. You saw something in this story that needed to be told and taught me to search for God's voice in me.

My parents, my family and my friends—
Thank you for an immeasurable amount of support, encouragement, prayer, and just being there for me to be my safe place so I could be myself. You may not have always known what was going on inside of me, but all of you were there on the outside for me. And after a very lonely, rocky and isolated path for nearly a decade I can now say that God has brought me friends. There have been countless cups of coffee, walks, lunches and prayers that I needed from all of you to tell me that I could do this.

*"I have personally experienced most of the emotions that Casey talks about in this book. I love her vulnerable transparency to show her true self to women just like myself trying to navigate ministry, motherhood and relationships. We need more women like Casey with a willing spirit to do whatever it takes to bring forth and encouraging word."*

Regan Frizzelle
Non-Profit Church Restored Foundation
Hope Fellowship Church, Frisco, TX

Dear Reader,

I am a reluctant writer. I'm a wife and a momma, and that's my focus in life. I love my family and I love my church. These are the things that matter to me. I did not write this book to *become* a writer, or make myself known. I wrote this book solely out of obedience to God. Very reluctantly.

Just like you'll find out later in this book, I am a leader that doesn't feel like a leader and now I am also a writer that doesn't feel like a writer. I'm just me. I am just here to help other people that are just *them*. Maybe you're hurting, asking why, and broken. God has pulled me out my most debilitating fears to echo powerful truths that have changed my life. It's okay to feel weak, and to struggle with wounds and fears.

My sole motive for writing this was to help those that are wounded and frozen in fear. I have prayed for you to find healing as you read this and for God to restore your calling through my story. Hurt, brokenness and isolation is so very common in our world, but stories are rarely shared because of shame and fear. You can bet I am fearful to share my story. It's vulnerable and real. It's hard to let people into your deepest fears and insecurities. I have done so, not with the motive of focusing on the hurt, but to focus on the Healer. I share this story so you don't feel alone any longer and you can see a way out of the pit.

I pray you learn to dream again and learn to lean into His Grace that is sufficient for you and His power that is made perfect in weakness.

Please share your story with me of finding His strength in your weakness and how God has put back together your broken pieces. He does that, you know. He puts us back together. And as I look back over all the pieces of my journey, every struggle I have had was part of His process that I needed. *And I am thankful for it all.*


With much love to you,
Casey

Share your story at -
Cgraves6@cox.net
www.weareperfectlyweak.com
www.facebook.com/CaseyGravesPerfectlyWeak

# Table of Contents

# Section One

## My Story

Chapter One

# Starting the Rest of My Life

I knew I wasn't living for the Lord. I knew I was ignoring His Call. I had pushed God far from the forefront of my mind. He was back there somewhere, but I had hidden Him and smothered the sound of His voice. I found it hard to pray, even though I did pray every night as I fell asleep. When I prayed, I felt so convicted knowing I wasn't actually allowing God to lead me, but rather asking for the generic blanket prayer of protection and help. It was a surface relationship between the two of us—God and I.

It wasn't always that way. I was raised in a home in which my grandfather was a pastor, my parents were deacons in their church, my mom played the organ and my dad taught Sunday School. We were at church every time the doors were open—Sunday morning, Sunday nights, Wednesday nights, and many times in between if necessary. I knew all the Bible stories and went to all the camps. I was set up to know God.

In fact, at one of those camps I felt called to be a pastor's wife. It was the summer I had just finished the eighth grade—going into high school—that I branched out of the normal camp routine, and joined Oak Cliff Assembly of God's youth group in their camp at South Padre Island. Sam Farina was the speaker, and I responded to an altar call about being called into the ministry. It was very real, and I remember it all very vividly. God and I were on this path together. Fast forward to age nineteen—back to the place I knew I wasn't living for the Lord. As I entered high school, I had allowed myself, like many teenagers, to get caught up in the world while leaving God out of the equation. I put more importance on friends, popularity, activities, sports, and boys than on God. I stopped asking Him what He wanted for my life and ignored His leading. Now, instead of pursuing a path to ministry, I was making decisions on where to go to college, what to major in, and what my life should look like. I had so many questions and very little peace.

I was lost. And I knew why. I also knew who could answer those questions for me—God. The God who had called me several years ago that I had pushed to the background. As I was struggling with all those questions, I was sitting in my backyard on a metal bench swing; staring and contemplating. I was so tired of being lost, so tired of living my life for me, and out of my own strength. I really wasn't sure if God even wanted to use me anymore like He had told me a few years back. But I could always feel Him tugging ever so slightly at me. So, I just sat there in silence, thinking about *maybe* asking Him what to do.

I didn't even have to ask. He is the God who sees, and He saw me sitting there and took that opportunity to speak to me, even though I didn't deserve it. As I sat there, it was as close to an audible voice as it could be that I heard. I heard so unmistakably clear the words, "If you don't get up now and fax your transcripts to Southwestern Assemblies of God University, then you are going to miss everything that I have planned for your life. Go." At that moment, God was letting me know that I needed to make that change, and quick.

It was July, which meant college was starting in a month. People usually enroll months before school starts. I had one month. That day God spoke, I literally jumped up, sent in my transcripts, and called the registrar to set up a college visit for that same week. I called my mom and told her she needed to take me to that college visit immediately. It was like something clicked inside me. It was the first obedience toward God I had in years. I was repentant, ready to listen, and on my way.

Not surprisingly, but miraculously, God worked out every single detail of moving to college in less than thirty days. I had a room in the dorm I wanted, with a roommate, classes scheduled, a major picked, and all my belongings packed. I was leaving for college. A whirlwind of change had occurred in my heart, just from those few, nearly audible, words God spoke to me. *Those words started the rest of my life.* And God's voice has saved me in many ways since then. He has pulled me out and put me right where He wanted me to be with His well-timed words.

On the very first day I moved into the dorm, I met my future husband—Justin. Talk about timing! I look back and realize that God said to me in the backyard if I didn't move fast, I was going to miss what He had for me. Things started happening quickly—although the first meeting with Justin was a little bumpy. I was in an all-girl dorm, and guys were only allowed in on the first couple of days to help with the move in process. I was at the end of the hall, and I could hear this guy going from room to room introducing himself, and talking with returning friends. He was taking this opportunity with the dorm open to get acquainted—or reacquainted, with all the girls. As I could hear him making his way down to my room, I was very skeptical of him by the time he got to me. He was so friendly, though, as he introduced himself to me. It was hard not to want to get to know him.

He left, and I continued to unpack and keep to myself. It's like I was instantly back on track. I was so focused on God and what He wanted. I would spend hours reading my Bible, honestly because I felt like I needed to catch up from not reading it for so long. I felt "behind" as I was at college with all of these church ministry majors that were on target with God (or so it seemed). But I was thankful to be right where God wanted me to be. God was always faithful even when I was not. It was good, and I was happy.

Attending this Bible University was the best thing that ever happened to me at this point in my life. My relationship with God flourished, I met friends that were headed in the same direction of ministry and spurred me on in my faith, and God grew my relationship with Justin there. Our first date was in October (after I had met him in August on that first day) for Homecoming. He had my roommate put tulips and a poem in my room inviting me on the date. Leading up to this, we had become great friends. He would knock on my window—which was way against the rules—and ask me to walk around the prayer walk area. He would take me to the post office, to Wal-Mart, and to dinner to introduce me to his friends. He had so many friends at college, and I came knowing no one. He was literally a lifesaver to me.

I was definitely scared of him at first. Not scared for my safety, but intimidated by his personality. I was shy, reserved, and very guarded, while he was overly obnoxious, over-the-top friendly, and full of fun. He was risky and I was cautious. But God used him to reach me. After that first date, which was a group date of about thirty friends to dinner and a coffee shop, we began our courtship of about two years. There were a few on again, off again moments—which were totally all his fault—but we made it and got engaged in March of his last semester of college.

He was a youth ministry major, and he was going to be an amazing youth pastor. He had an intense heart for evangelism with passion for the lost that challenged me, love for teenagers, and the required energy and creativity needed for a job like that. As he was starting his last semester of college, and we got engaged, he took a part-time job at a church that was within driving distance of our university.

Our dating life had been magical to me. Justin was very romantic and so much fun—always outdoing himself with creative dates. We did everything together - study at coffee shops, walk around different college campuses, have picnics at the park, ride roller coasters at amusement parks, baseball games, etc. I was floating on this high from my renewed relationship with God and our college dating life, but real life was about to hit.

Chapter Two

# Brokenness Began

*God can restore what is broken and turn it into something amazing.*

I was twenty-one and he was twenty-two, he had just graduated from college and we were engaged. We were young, excited, passionate about ministry, and naïve. Naïve is the key part here. What we experienced in ministry was not what we expected. We expected our magical world we had created in college to continue. We were hard workers, willing to roll up our sleeves to serve, but there was so much more we didn't know. We hadn't yet experienced betrayal, cynicism, criticism, and hurt—but we were about to.

Ministry is much more than what people see on Sundays. It is not just the thrill of watching God change people's lives right in front of you. It's not just the privilege of being used to minister to someone in their time of need. It's hard. It's facing opposition, listening to criticism about your spouse who is just a person that needs direction and mentoring, but is met with harshness. It has moments (sometimes several and often) that can feel the opposite of what you'd think it would feel when people don't believe in you, or question your integrity and character when you've given them your whole heart. It was definitely being thrown into the deep end for us.

At our first church where we ministered, we were deeply wounded. We only lasted three months there, after we were married. We were in a situation where Justin was pushed to be a workaholic. He and the staff worked from very early morning through late nights on a regular basis. While he is not against working hard, this was over the top and very difficult on us as newlyweds. There would be days in a row that I didn't see him at all.

After a considerable amount of this kind of working, we decided that we couldn't hack it in ministry. If this was what ministry was, we couldn't do it. We thought that maybe we had missed God in our calling. We were questioning everything we thought our life would be. We were already burned out and weren't willing to sacrifice our marriage, so we decided to resign. We weren't looking for another ministry position elsewhere, we were just giving up.

The craziest thing happened at that moment. We were in Justin's office when we made our final decision to quit, and the phone rang. It was a friend from college that lived a few hours away that wanted us to interview at their church to be their youth pastor. No one knew we were quitting. No one, except God. We were in the deep end, but not without a life raft.

We didn't really know what to say—because we still felt like ministry may not be for us. We knew we were called, but we were wavering with serious doubts. Justin was always the one willing to take the risk and agreed to the interview.

Again, being naïve, we went to discuss these events with our pastor—expecting some encouragement. When we shared our struggles with him, he began to tell us that we could never cut it in ministry and we did not have what it takes to make it long term if we couldn't make it there at his church. He said he would not accept our resignation and he gave us two weeks to pray about it.

We were stunned. This was our pastor—a position that we held in high esteem. His words held weight in our eyes. His opinion mattered to us. What he said crushed us. We were reeling after that conversation, yet decided to still head to the interviews at the next church. After the two weeks passed, we resigned from our current church, with the reason of taking a new position in a different town.

This seemed like a colossal failure to me. To make it worse, we were instructed to leave right away that week. We were asked to attend one last Thanksgiving event, but we were not to tell anyone we were moving. We were not allowed to have a youth service to tell the teenagers that we ministered to goodbye and we were instructed to just disappear. We knew this was wrong. We knew this would hurt and damage so many of those kids we had loved. It would seem to them that we never loved them at all.

We wrestled with following those instructions. We wanted to tell people the truth. We wanted to tell people goodbye, and to let the youth group know we did love them and care for them. But we also knew we needed to be respectful to the leader of that church. We called Justin's pastor/mentor and asked for advice. He advised us to honor the pastor's wishes and quietly leave without causing a stink. That was one of the hardest things to do in my life because I knew it would hurt so many people.

This was before email, texting, and social media. No one could track us down and ask questions. We weren't able to contact people and tell them we really did love them and weren't heartless cowards that just abandoned them. We just vanished.

Years later after we moved, we bumped into someone from that church in our new location. They began to tell us how our resignation letter that the pastor had read to the church after we left didn't sound like us. It said that we had left for a bigger church with higher pay. Our stomachs sunk. We did not write a resignation letter, and did not leave under those circumstances.

I don't share this story to bash any church or person. I share this story to explain the journey of brokenness that began very early on in our ministry. A journey that is shared by many (I dare say most) in full-time ministry, volunteer ministry—or any kind of ministry for that matter. You don't have to be a pastor's wife to have encountered similar pain. However, the focus is not the damage done by people and situations, but on the Healer who can restore and rebuild what is broken in our lives.

God has not spared us from pain and rejection in our ministry, but has used it to refine us and prepare us to propel forward in His service. Every single hurt that we have experienced has been used by God because all things work together for the good of those who love Him and are called according to His purposes. We have seen that verse proven true, over and over in our lives.

During the difficult times, I have asked God "why" so many times. Why did he allow me to be hurt so often? But as I look back on it all, I wouldn't trade any experiences, because they have molded and shaped me into the person I am—a person that is way more dependent on God and more usable than that twenty-one year old who started out ready to take on the world. Now I know I can't take on the world, but God can through me.

Though grace has met me at every turn, there were several more years and experiences after that first one that chipped away at my confidence, and left me hesitant to open up and be myself. I had been on the receiving end of criticism and personal attacks enough times to harbor mistrust toward most people. There were many prayers that I felt were unanswered, though God always answered in His own way.

While I briefly started out strong, my calling and my hope dwindled to where all I could see was broken dreams. I have wanted to give up over and over again. I had become the sum total of my weaknesses. I had yet to learn to be perfectly weak—allowing His strength to be perfected in me no matter what.

Chapter Three

# The End of Me and The Beginning of God's Dream

Years had passed – nine to be exact—and we were at our fourth church to hold the position of youth pastor. That adds up to many youth camps, six flags trips, and lock-ins! I was worn from the years of ministry, not filling myself up with the Lord like I needed. I had become a mom of two babies, and was tired; spiritually and physically. It was a normal day in our house just before Christmas—full of expectation for the holidays, but still a week or two before the celebration started. The house was decorated and both of our children were awake. Chloe, our six-month-old, was in the swing. Charli, our three-year-old, was looking at the ornaments on our tree and trying hard not to touch them. Dinner was ready and we were in the living room looking at the Christmas tree when we heard the garage door open. Charli and I got really excited and she squealed, "Daddy's home!" and ran to greet him at the back door. Justin scooped her into his arms and joined us by the tree. After playing with the girls for a few minutes, he told me we needed to talk. I noticed the tone in his voice was different than usual.

Then, with the children still playing, he just plainly said, "I got fired today." I looked at him to make sure he wasn't joking, because Justin is a very funny person and always loves a good joke. But he was just standing there next to the fireplace—with our Christmas stockings hanging from the mantle and the tree and all our decorations in place—just looking at me with a very solemn expression on his face. "I'm serious," he said. "I got fired today." I didn't know what to think.

Almost from the beginning of our ministry together, Justin had sensed God calling him to plant a church and we felt like his position at the church where he was working would be the next step toward that ultimate goal. We left our previous position to come there in hopes of learning more about the church planting process, but things had not been easy. Justin had been struggling. I had, too. And our finances were in desperate shape. That day, just before Christmas, when he told me he'd been fired, we were broke. With two children to care for, we could barely afford groceries and gas. It was not exactly what we thought ministry would be like almost ten years earlier when we first began. So, facing this new difficult experience, much of the hurt and pain we'd experienced before came bubbling to the surface.

Throughout the fall of that year, we were praying and seeking God for help with our situation. Like I said, we were just barely scraping by financially, so our prayers were often for things like a Christmas bonus or a raise. We were feeling desperate, but trying to have faith and believe that God would come through for us. Then Justin came home with the news that he'd lost his job. At Christmas. With a new baby. And we were broke. That really wasn't the answer to prayer that we expected.

Justin grinned and said, "Well, we were asking God to do something, I guess this is His answer."

Looking back now, it was the exact answer we needed, but right then it didn't feel like it. I wasn't freaked out –yet. That happened later. We were just stunned...and relieved. But even with that strange hint of relief, we knew whatever was ahead was not going to be easy either.

The next month was a blur of mixed emotions from relief, to anger, to every range of turmoil. I was so angry at how everything had happened in my life. I was angry about leaving church, leaving friends, and moving. I was in an awful place that could only see hurt.

Rather quickly after that, Justin began talking about planting a church in Tulsa. We had lived in Tulsa previously and had often dreamed of planting a church there. I had been interested in that, too, when we were first married but after almost ten years of hardship in ministry, I was at my breaking point. I was done with ministry. Although I knew with my mind that we were called to start a church, right then I didn't really care anymore. I was tired of being hurt in ministry. I just couldn't take it anymore. I wanted out.

Aside from being hurt, we had no obvious means of starting a church. We had no sponsors, no people, and absolutely no money. How would we even begin? It was way too scary for me and I was way too wounded to begin. I told Justin how I felt repeatedly, yet he kept talking about starting the church as if I had agreed to do it. As if he knew, deep inside, what he was called to do and knew it so convincingly he was certain it would happen. I, deep down inside really,

*really* did not want to start that church...or be a pastor's wife anymore.

And yet, while feeling and saying all that to Justin, I still could hear God whispering to me. Talking to me. He was reminding me of my calling. I dismissed His voice and tried to ignore Him, but He kept coming back.

One night as I was lying in bed crying while Justin was asleep, I heard God very clearly say, "If you will just be willing, I will do the rest." He wanted me to say yes. That's all I had to do. And at the moment, saying yes to Him was the hardest thing I could do. It was actually physically hard for me to get the word out. But lying there that night, I said yes to God in the faintest whisper I could muster. I meant it, but I didn't feel it.

I still felt overwhelmed, angry, hurt, and scared. I did not want to start that church. But I had decided that if God asked me to be willing, then I could do that and I was going to watch Him keep His end of the bargain and let Him do the rest—because I couldn't.

As I mentioned, I felt totally alone with no friends or supports of any kind, but a friend who learned of Justin's interest in starting a church agreed to help. So, while I worried about what to do and where to live—we couldn't stay where we were—Justin headed off to a church-planting boot camp. I stayed home to take care of all the daily details—caring for the girls, packing our home, and finding a house that we could buy in Tulsa.

Our house where we'd been living sold on Valentine's Day. I am a sentimental person and I love holidays. I felt like Christmas that year was ruined because we had to put our house on the market—we listed it on Christmas Eve—and now Valentine's Day was ruined because our house sold on that day. I know that sounds odd, most people celebrate when their house sells, but emotionally that's where I was right then. I was mad at Justin because we had to move, mad because we had to sell, and mad because it sold. That reaction made no sense to the reasonable part of my mind—it wasn't Justin's fault it all worked out that way. In fact, it was nothing less than a miracle that our house sold that quickly. And somewhere deep inside, I knew that God was already working on our behalf, holding up His end of the agreement we made that night, but I wasn't ready to see past the hurt I still felt inside. I was sinking deeper into all these feelings of despair. Most days, I didn't bother to change from my sweatpants and hoodie.

And still, we had to move to Tulsa. So, while Justin was away, I left the house—dressed in sweatpants and hoodie—and headed to the library to use their computers to search for a house.

Being newly unemployed with no verifiable source of income, except *possible* donations that may or may not come in and the *hope* that we would start a church in a year, it was impossible to get a loan. So, my search for a house to buy quickly turned into a search for a house to rent. That search proved difficult as well.

From previously living in the Tulsa area, we knew which part of the city we wanted to live in and the schools we wanted our girls to attend, but there were no houses for rent in that area. The longer I looked the more discouraged I became, but I kept at it and finally came across one house— just one—that was listed for lease. I called the rental company and the agent told me there was already a pending rental agreement on the home, but if I moved fast and faxed him my rental application quickly we could be considered. So I moved fast. We had a good credit history, but with no money and no job I didn't expect the rental to workout.

Filling out the application went rather quickly. Gathering the supporting documents and information took a little longer. But as soon as I sent the last of the paperwork, the agent called me and said we were approved for the house. I couldn't believe it. That was the first good news I had heard in a long time. God was beginning to move, and I could see my first glimmer of hope.

Thinking about it now, a logical response might have been to give thanks, repent of my unbelief, and move forward boldly with our plans. That's the typical kind of thing you hear from many sermons. But that wasn't my reaction. Very quickly I focused on the opposite. We had a home, but we also had a monthly rental payment that had to be met. And we still had no money to pay it.

After learning about the house, I went home that day and sat down to write our first ministry letter asking for financial support and prayer partners for our church plant. I wasn't writing out of newfound passion for planting, but rather out of how-am-I-going-to-pay-for-rent panic.

Those first envelopes and letters were handwritten—we had no computer—and I sent them to everyone I knew, family, close friends, and anyone with whom we had a relationship in ministry. I felt embarrassed, awkward and apologetic asking for money. Inside, I knew it wasn't really for me but for the church we were trying to plant, but I hated writing those letters. With each letter I thought, "Who is going to read this and send us enough money to make even a small dent in what we need to fund a church and staff members?" I could see no way for any of this to workout.

## Perfectly Weak

Yet, despite my skepticism, money started to come in. And the cool part was, the money didn't come from our relatives. It came from unexpected sources. From people we were not close to and from some whom we would never have expected to support us.

God was on the move. I was still worried.

Chapter Four

# In the Cave —
# I Couldn't Get Beyond My
# Circumstances

With our first donation we bought a laptop. Then one of our friends bought cell phones for us just before we moved. We didn't have enough money to purchase them ourselves and he knew we would need them as we relocated and began to plant the church.

The day we moved, my parents came up to help us. My mom helped me drive our girls to the new house while Justin, my dad, and some friends—who refused to be disconnected from us in spite of all that happened—packed our belongings into a U-Haul truck. I was nervous about the move, going to a new neighborhood, in a new city—and because we had signed the rental agreement for our new home without seeing it first. We had seen pictures of the house on the internet, but had not visited the property or toured the house. It sounds crazy but it was the only house available when we filed the application, and there wasn't time to see it first. We just took it. But as moving day approached and then as we made the trip to Tulsa, I was worried.

Mom and I drove to Tulsa with the girls and made our way into this new neighborhood. Justin and I didn't know anyone who lived there and even though we wanted to live there, we had never actually spent time in this area of town before. But as I drove up to our new home, I was pleasantly surprised. It was newly constructed and clean. We'd never lived in a new home before. Yet there we were, in Tulsa, in a new house, still standing. We made it out alive, but that sense of satisfaction didn't last long.

In a little while, Justin and my dad arrived with the truck and we began unloading. As we moved in, I had a sinking feeling in my stomach as questions started pouring into my mind. Where were we going to go to church while we worked on starting ours? Where would we find people to help us? And as those questions piled up I began to feel really alone again.

Adjusting to the move was difficult for me, but Justin took this move as an exciting challenge. He was ready. The first thing he did was get a job. Then, he started looking for a location for us to hold our church services.

That first job was at Starbucks, which not only provided an income but also health insurance. Having a toddler and an infant meant lots of doctor visits, so insurance was a big concern. We were receiving some donations, but not enough to pay for that on our own. So Justin went to work at Starbucks at four in the morning every day and got off by noon so he could make appointments to meet with people about the church.

We also located a church to attend while we were developing the one we wanted to plant. It was a big church with a well-established congregation, but as we walked into that beautiful sanctuary and placed our children in their amazing children's ministry, my heart sank. I said to myself, "Can't we just stay here? This is safe. This building is already built and paid for, and they have a children's ministry for my kids." I just wanted so badly to be safe, not risky. I wanted to be comfortable.

While I wanted to stay at this safe and comfortable church, Justin was searching through options for venues where we could hold our church services. He checked with movie theaters, other churches, and schools in the area but it seemed every place that he wanted was unavailable. He was praying big prayers for a big and visible building. What we got was an old, stinky school that was hidden, small, and not visible at all. It was the only place available.

Justin said at the time, "The only people driving down the road this school is on are people who drive there on purpose." And he was right. No one accidentally drove past that school. Which meant no one would casually see our church sign. It was a terrible location, or so we thought.

Even though God was moving, I still was struggling. We had moved into the rental house which was really great, in the neighborhood where we'd wanted to live, which was wonderful, but on a practical, daily basis all I could see was rows and rows of houses filled with people I didn't know, in an area with which I was unfamiliar. We'd lived there before but that was five years earlier. Now I felt foggy and lost. We were driving two cars that needed new transmissions. I spent most of my day with our ten-month old and three-year old, whom I loved with all my heart and for whom I wanted the best, but I'd been crushed and hurt by the last nine years of ministry experiences. And there we were, moving forward with planting a church that I still did not want to be a part of. It was all too much for me. And I still was angry.

I knew God was there. I talked to Him every day, but I was angry with Him and didn't understand why He allowed hurtful things to happen to me. I knew He was sovereign. I knew He was in control of everything. But rather than bringing a sense of peace and reassurance, the thought of His power and authority only made me mad, mostly because I knew life didn't have to happen to us the way it did. He could have made things turn out different. But He didn't. I cringed when well-meaning people would say things like, "God has a reason for everything," or "God uses all things for good in our lives." I knew those sentiments were true, but I was years away from being ready to digest them. I was terribly disappointed at where we were in life after almost ten years of marriage.

So, one day I began to tell God that I was angry, which was nothing new. I'd been telling Him that same thing every day for quite a while. This time, however, I began to tell Him that not only did we not have things we *needed*, but that I couldn't see any way we could ever have anything we *wanted* or see any of our dreams come true. They were dreams God had given us, but I had given up—for real this time. I was done. It all seemed impossible and every day I let Him know how I felt.

But even after saying all that to Him, God kept whispering to me, "If you will just be willing, I will do the rest." So I got up every day and said the words, "I am willing." I said it, but I didn't feel it. I so desperately wanted those feelings to come as we planted this church. I wanted to feel the joy and excitement about this journey that Justin felt—it was difficult to watch Justin and see his excitement every day about what we were doing and all the while I was so angry. But day after day, in spite of my prayers, nothing changed. So, I kept going and just took one step at a time.

When God asked, I'd said I was willing. So, when we began holding worship services, that meant I had to show up for church every Sunday to set up, run the preschool ministry, and tear it all down afterward. I got pretty good at that, because I am a doer and not a dreamer. And because it gave me a place to hide. Also, I had a vested interest in making the preschool ministry good because I had two preschoolers of my own who were part of the program. I was worried they might hate having to attend church in a high school band room as much as I did. And I was concerned they would have no friends to join them in their children's church. I shouldn't have been afraid. God did not disappoint. People showed up and the children's ministry began to grow, as I continued to hide. Afraid of being hurt. Afraid to step into the role He had for me. I was wounded, and I responded by focusing on the wounds —and not the Healer—which meant I was disabling myself from stepping into the leadership He was calling me toward. *I had to learn you can't recognize the God of the impossible inside of you, while dwelling on the negative circumstances around you.*

––––––

The process of planting the church was marked with miracle after miracle. God took care of us through every decision we faced. He knew what we needed before we even asked. When we didn't even know what we needed or wanted, God knew. After we had rented our house for a year, we were looking for a small, older home to buy. By then the church was up and running and our income was fairly steady, so we were hoping that we would be able to qualify for a loan this time.

Our friend, John, was a homebuilder in Tulsa. A contract for one of his newly constructed houses fell through and the house had been sitting empty for more than a year. John had approached us about buying the house when we moved to Tulsa a year earlier. We respectfully declined then because it was way out of our price range. Now, a year later, I was looking at houses we could afford and Justin started talking about John's house, wondering if it was still available. I knew we couldn't afford that house and dismissed the idea of buying it without a second thought, but Justin called him anyway.

John knew our situation so when he asked Justin what we could afford, Justin told him our price range and the kind of monthly payment we could make. To our shock and amazement, John didn't flinch—or laugh. Instead, he took the information to his partners. Not long after that, they sold us the house for the amount Justin had said we could afford, which was considerably less than their own cost to build it. And after everything was in place, our monthly mortgage payment was exactly the same as our rent payment had been.

In addition to that, after we had been in the out-of-the-way school building for three years, setting up and tearing down an entire church every Sunday, people from a church down the street paid us a visit. Their congregation was growing older and had lost so many members they couldn't afford their church building anymore. As a result, the congregation wanted to dissolve. Because their building was located about a mile from where we'd been meeting, they had driven past us almost daily and had seen our church signs. They had received offers to sell their property to real estate developers who wanted it for apartment complexes and parking lots, but they knew we needed a building and they wanted their building to continue to be used to reach people for Jesus. So, unbeknownst to us, they attended our services a few times to see who we were and what we were doing, then approached Justin about the possibility of buying their building.

Although our congregation was growing and getting stronger every week, we weren't at a place where we could afford to buy a building like theirs, but Justin talked to them anyway. As you might expect by now, they ended up selling us their building for way less than its appraised value, and they sold it to us at a cost we could afford to pay.

And there we were, living in Tulsa, in a new house, with our church in a big building visible from the highway. We would never have been given that big and visible building—which Justin had prayed for from the beginning—if we had not started at the school we thought was such a bad location. And we wouldn't have received a new house if we hadn't rented the other one first, or made the move, or…as difficult as it is to admit…if Justin hadn't been fired. God was at work in our lives, and He was answering prayers, just not like we thought He should.

I want to use the rest of this book as kind of a step-by-step guide of how to allow God to build His Dream into your life. This book is from my perspective…as a pastor's wife and church planter. The stories and examples reflect my experience, but can be applied to whatever dream it is that God is calling out of you. You don't have to be pastor, church planter, or in full-time vocational ministry to build God's Dream into your life. You just have to be willing, and being willing, usually means taking a risk.

## Perfectly Weak

With each risk I have taken, God has changed me. I am different now than when we planted our church, or even when we began in ministry. God has changed me from fearful to confident, from jealous to loving, from thinking and speaking words of death to words of life. God has fulfilled promises in my life that I have only seen because I jumped out into the deep end for Him. He does this when we obey Him, step out of our comfort zones, and risk for Him.

Section Two

# What it Takes to Build God's Dream Into Your Life

Chapter Five

# It Takes Risk

*"An adventure will make you late for dinner."*
*- Bilbo Baggins in The Hobbit*

Our fledgling church continued to grow, God did not disappoint us. While I was willing, He did the rest just like He said He would. He continued to bring the increase we needed. When I looked at what was happening, how the congregation had expanded, and all that had occurred since we began, I knew God was working according to His plan for us. But I still was struggling personally and I continued to hide from His calling. As I would discover, God had a plan for that, too.

Not long after we moved the congregation from the school to the church building a few blocks away, Justin preached a sermon about hiding. The message was based on the story of Goliath taunting the army of Israel to send someone out to fight him. Goliath was easily twice the size of the biggest Hebrew male and rather than taking the risk of meeting that challenge, the Israelite soldiers ran away and hid in their tents. Even with God on their side, and knowing all that He had done for them and for their ancestors in the past,

27

they were scared and refused to believe He would act on their behalf once more. Instead, they surrendered to fear and refused to face the giant. It took a young, overlooked shepherd boy named David, to defeat this giant.

In spite of the odds against him, but filled with faith and confidence, David accepted Goliath's challenge and went out to fight him, armed with only a sling and a few rocks. You know the end of the story. David won and not only defeated the giant, but went on to become king of the entire nation.

The main point of the sermon was how we are a lot like those soldiers. Instead of allowing God to use us and fight through us, instead of stepping into His calling—no matter how risky it might appear at the beginning—we have a tendency to run away and hide.

When I heard the sermon, I knew it was for me. I realized that was exactly what I was doing—hiding from the giant of fear. In fact, hiding from many such giants. Fear that I would be hurt again, fear that things wouldn't work out at the church and we'd have to go through all of the pain again; fear that God wouldn't do what He said He would do, fear I wouldn't be a good leader.

For two more years I went through the motions of being involved. I did everything in my power to avoid meaningful contact with those who attended the church. It was difficult to engage with other adults because I was scared. Our children were young so I continued to teach in the children's ministry on Sunday morning, but as soon as church was over, I got out of the way and out of the classroom with as little adult interaction as possible.

At the Sunday morning worship service, I sat in the back of the sanctuary—literally on the back row—and if I felt uncomfortable or sensed that someone might approach me when the service concluded, I scooted out early and went home. I was hiding from being a leader. I wasn't growing in the position in which God had placed me, or accepting this new challenge. I was choosing to stay hidden and comfortable.

Not only was I not growing into the leadership position God had given me as a teacher and as a pastor's wife, I wasn't growing personally either. Strange as it may seem, as much as I might have said I wanted to get beyond those hurts of the past, the pain of those previous experiences was comfortable. It was something with which I was familiar and wallowing in it required no effort at all on my part. So, I coddled the pain from those previous experiences and used it to justify taking the easy way out. And God let me—for a while. He's so gracious. He let me hide and be comfortable. Because for the time being, all He needed was for me to be willing. He knew what I could handle and allowed me time to heal.

After two years of this hiding, I began to feel God tapping me on the head and saying, "You can do more." I ignored those nudges and each time dismissed them with a firm, "No, I cannot!" He continued to prompt me, but I continued to tell Him things like, "This is good. Let me just stay here comfortably. Let me stay right here on the back row, as far from others as possible. I can't do more."

God persisted and slowly that light tap from Him grew more constant and more insistent. As I refused to get out of my comfort zone, that quiet voice that first said, "You can do more," grew to a louder and more pronounced banging on my head and heart saying, "I *need* you to get up and do more." And then, as I heard that day in my parent's back yard when I was procrastinating about college, He said in an unmistakable shout, "I need you to do more. Get up and get moving!"

I was terrified; completely paralyzed with fear. I didn't think I could do more. I didn't want to do more. I was afraid of ministry and people by this point that I had allowed myself to become frozen into fear. But, while I was hiding, and ignoring God, I still knew I was called. I had this dream barely flickering so deep inside that I could hardly acknowledge it. Deep down, those passionate feelings to lead people to Jesus and minister to the hurting were still there. I was afraid to acknowledge them.

I really didn't want to go through life missing out on what God wanted to do in me. *But what could I do?* I really felt like a big bunch of nothing. I had completely lost any dream I had ever dreamed. I had lost all self-confidence and bravery. I was in this cold, fearful place, hiding. But I could hear him calling.

I had said yes that night, right before Christmas, when we were in the throes of leaving the church where Justin was fired, and I knew I had to respond again. So I looked for ways God was asking me to step out of my comfort zone. Simple ways. Easy ways. Some small baby steps I could take to respond to God.

Some of the first things I did were internal and not easily seen by others—like listening to God and stepping out to talk with a particular person that God spoke to me about, or praying with someone as I felt led.

Other things I did were more obvious, like standing in the lobby to greet people, leading small groups, leading women's Bible studies—which meant studying and preparing more. I also took steps to launch and direct our women's ministry. All of these things included teaching, organizing women and events, working with others, and putting myself out there. Doing all of that stretched me even further.

Each step led to another and with each step I asked God for the strength and grace I needed to get through it. I was desperately relying on Him and heavily leaning on Him, which was so much better than relying on myself.

Now, this will sound a little ridiculous to some but one of the biggest things I did was to change the place where I sat during the worship service. I moved from the back row to the front. I know that sounds really silly now—but for me that was really putting myself out there. I could literally hide in the back and always had the option of sneaking out if I needed to—not that I ever had to, but the option was there. Sitting in front made me feel vulnerable—up there for all to see. It felt safer for me in the back.

Gradually, however, sitting up front became more comfortable. Sitting next to my husband was a small way for me to support him and acknowledge that I was called, alongside him, to pastor this church and lead with him. To me, it was the ultimate act of crawling out of my cave.

As much as I feared being hurt again by church members, I was also afraid of speaking in public. I would have rather done anything—wash the dishes, clean the bathroom, organize events behind the scenes—anything other than that. But I realized that if God was continuing to pull me out further from hiding, I was going to have to do things that made me afraid, and about the time I came to that realization Justin started asking me to speak on different occasions like Mother's Day, tag-team preaching about marriage, or at some of our women's events.

In my head, my initial response to those requests was always "no." But since I knew God was asking me to step up,

I said "yes," and then panicked. Then I noticed another thing happening. As I began to do more at the church, more was asked of me—not just about speaking but about any number of things—and rather than shrink back from it, I did my best to lean into it. I got to the point where anytime someone asked me to do something that made me nervous or fearful, I immediately took the risk and said yes. Having caught a glimpse of what life was like on the other side of fear—which was trust in God—I wasn't going to let fear hold me back anymore.

And along the way, something really amazing and exciting happened. I began to dream again. Against all of my reservations, all of my fear, and all the past experiences of hurt, I let God in. I allowed Him into my mess, and included Him in all of the vulnerability I had surrounding my insecurity. He brought me to a place where I could say yes to more than just to being willing—reluctantly willing—but to dreaming again and to actually believing that God could use me.

After I began to dream again, I realized my dreams were the same as all those years in ministry before, yet different. I began to forgive those who hurt me, and embrace the journey that we had been on, even though I never agreed to all the heartache and always thought God could've prevented some of the pain. The last ten years in ministry could've been easier, if easier was the point. Those years didn't have to go the way they did. But now I realized I had to be broken. There were many things in my life that had to be swept away so that God could transform me into the person He wanted me to be and those painful experiences, as excruciating as they might have been, were the only way to clear from my life the things that were holding me back—things which, at the time, I was not even aware of.

In the first few years of ministry, I was full of confidence and dreams of what the future would be like, but somewhere along the way I began to think they were *my* dreams and plans and God *owed me* the fulfillment of them. I wanted things to happen *my* way and when things didn't go the way I thought they should, I viewed it as God disappointing me. My perspective was "off," and it was wrong. To deal with that wrong attitude and perspective, God had to take me to the point where all my dreams were crushed—and they were—so He could give me *His* dreams. God never owed me anything. I owed Him my life.

It's easy for us to get our perspective off of God and onto ourselves, and what we want. I had to be realigned with God's purposes, not my own, even though those purposes were ministry based. The dream God had to repurpose in my heart was to solely bring glory to God, and to love others, not self. I had to be reconnected with the simple remembrance that He saved me and if I was left to my own devices I was lost and dying.

The crushing of my dreams eventually led to my renewed realization and focus on how He saved my life in so many ways and how He was my source of all things—from salvation all the way down to rent and grocery money. I had unintentionally gotten to a place where my purpose was backwards and had the subtle wrong thinking *that He is here for us, instead of we are here for Him.* I had to get back to the place where God could create in me a clean heart, and restore in me the dreams in which He created me for. Instead of praying and believing that He was supposed to answer *my* prayers, and do what *I* wanted, I would now ask God what He wanted and do my best to please Him and not please myself. I had come to a place of being willing to answer His Call with no expectation of receiving anything. Doing that involved confronting one of the things I was avoiding most—risk.

To be engaged—fully engaged in that kind of dream and calling in life—I had to take the risk that I might be misunderstood. Someone might get the wrong impression of me. Things might not work out and situations might just fall apart. Love extended to someone might not be returned. Worse yet, we might be intentionally hurt. If that was possible, I still struggled with that kind of risk.

I had learned to respond to hurt not by passionately pursuing the dynamic and life-giving will of God, but ordering my life instead after *my* ideas of what was safe. I may have started out naïve and idealistic with those dynamic, God-inspired dreams, but the hurt and struggle of ministry quickly hampered all that and I responded by turning inward. To turn me back toward the dreams God had for me, He had to change the way I thought.

That was painful and it took a while for me to see that all the things we encountered—those hurtful early ministry experiences, Justin losing his job, moving to Tulsa, renting a house sight-unseen, and launching the church in what seemed like the worst possible location—was actually God hard at work in our lives to give us—to give me—the desires of our heart. Not even the desires I could articulate in prayers. What God wanted to give me were the dreams that lay deep down inside. Dreams for which He had created me. Dreams I hardly recognized were there.

The first risk I confronted was simply the risk of saying yes. When we say yes to God, we're actually saying, "I'm putting my desires aside, and giving you control. Whatever

34

you want, Lord, even if I don't understand it, I'm willing to do it." It's a gamble to our finite minds—like handing the dice to God and letting him do the roll. That's about how it felt to me. I was trusting someone else with the safety and well-being of myself and my family, after already experiencing hurt and disappointment that I didn't understand. I was trusting Him with everything. And that is scary, because I knew it might not turn out the way I wanted it to. I had to trust that it would turn out the way God wanted it to, and know that His way is better, even if I couldn't see how.

That's the place I had to get to in order to be ready for God to build His Dream into my life.

A friend of ours often says, "You can't see the beauty and wonder of the Grand Canyon from the safety of the paved road. You have to get all the way up to the edge and lean over the rail." That's what our journey has been like. It felt like we were hanging off the edge of a cliff, holding on to the barest thread of a lifeline that might break at any minute. What we had to learn—and what we still are learning—was that God held the other end of that line and He wasn't about to let us fall.

Chapter Six

# It Takes Welcoming Weakness

*My grace is sufficient for you, for my power is made*
*perfect in weakness. Therefore, I will boast all the more*
*gladly about my weaknesses so that Christ's power may rest*
*on me. That is why, for Christ's sake, I delight in weaknesses,*
*in insults, in hardships, in persecutions and in difficulties,*
*because when I am weak, then I am strong.*
*2 Corinthians 12:9-10 (NIV)*

When I was at my lowest point, I actually said to my husband, "We are done. We are going to be those people who just barely survive. We won't live out any of our dreams or do any of the things we wanted to do. And we'll struggle our whole lives just to get by." And I meant it. From the very core of my being, I had given up. We were at a place where we could do nothing at all to change our circumstances. I was raised to be a strong, confident, smart, determined, tough person, but at my lowest point, I was completely broken.

For me, that was my worst place, but for God and His purposes, I was in the best place I'd ever been in my life. He was ready to put me back together and mold me into someone He could actually use. And when I gave up, God came in.

## Perfectly Weak

Now, I was usable, but also intensely alerted of how weak I was.

Being exposed to risk—the kind that leaves you wondering if life will go on—exposes our weakness. As I began to step out and obey God, I was now keenly aware that I had so many weaknesses. My experiences combined with my new willingness to take a risk for God exposed all the areas in which I felt vulnerable. I felt like the least equipped person to do what God was asking of me, and still do at times. I was so focused on all the things I was not good at as a pastor's wife—I couldn't sing, play in the worship band, or speak eloquently at worship services—and I tended to be nervous and timid. I didn't have that bubbly personality that commands attention when I entered a room. I could only see everything I wasn't, instead of seeing all of what God is. While being focused on all that I *couldn't* do, I was missing out on all the God *could* do in me. As I, ever so slightly, stepped out in faith and actually did what He'd asked me to do, even though it was one baby step at a time, He started showing me what *He could do.*

I also noticed that rather than asking me to do the things I knew I could handle—like working behind the scenes, organizing and serving with little or no public attention—God kept asking me to do the things I knew I wasn't good at—like speaking, leading and teaching. My immediate response was, "I can't do that God. I'm so inadequate in those areas." At other times I said, "What if people don't like what I do because I am not good at it?" And there was the question I'd been asking since we began planting the church, "Why me? Why did you choose me?" Finally, God answered and said, "Because you said yes. Because you were willing."

God doesn't need our expertise. He needs our willingness to obey. To do what He asks us to do. He needs people who are willing to follow His dream even when that plan doesn't seem like much of a dream at all. He does not ask us to be over-the-top talented, gifted, and confident. He just needs willing hearts. I am nothing special. I was just willing to say yes.

When I first had the idea to write this book, I was too afraid to take the risk to begin. I argued about it with God for two years because I was focused solely on the things I didn't know and the skills I didn't have— saying I'm not a good writer, I don't have anything to say that people will want to read, I don't have time. Instead of just turning on the computer and typing, I gave well-rehearsed excuses about my weaknesses and my inabilities to God.

When I remained focused on what I couldn't do and on my weaknesses, I couldn't see what *He is in me*. I was limiting God and not allowing Him to work through me. When I finally gave up fighting God about writing, I decided to walk in a principle that Justin has preached about many times. This principle is the notion that you don't have to know *how* to do what God asks you to do, but you just have to know *what* God is asking you to do. Our job is to listen to what God asks us to do, and then be willing to act. It's His job to show us how and to make a way. We don't have to rely solely on our strengths—the things we think we are good at. We can rely on Him.

Oftentimes, we only consent to do things God asks us to do that we think we *can* do. Many times He will ask us to do things we can't do. I call those God-sized tasks. He doesn't want to call us to do things we can accomplish in our own power. He wants to use us to do things only He can do through us, in His power.

As a first step in applying that principle, I did the very thing I mentioned above. I turned on my computer and began to type. It didn't seem like much at first but before long I was totally absorbed by the task.

My desire to write quickly became noticeable and before long our daughters began to ask about it. "Mom, when will your book be finished? Mom, how does your book get printed and put on a bookshelf?" To each of those questions I said, "I don't know. I'm just supposed to write it and God will do the rest." Then I told them, "It's like everything else. I don't really know how to do anything I do. I just take it one step at a time."

And that's true. I don't know how to raise two daughters, be a pastor's wife or write a book, but God does, so I have to listen to Him. I can operate in those areas in which I feel lacking, by allowing God to work through me in His strength.

Paul writes in 2 Corinthians 12:9-10 the perfect scriptures to describe this process in me. It says, "My grace is sufficient for you, for my power is made perfect in weakness." That's a counter-intuitive concept—power through weakness. Most of us think that power comes through strength. That's certainly what the world tells us.

But Paul, having caught a glimpse of the idea God was trying to convey, went on to say, "Therefore I will boast all the more gladly in my weakness, so that Christ's power may rest on me. That is why, for Christ's sake, I delight in weaknesses, in insults, in hardships, in persecutions, in difficulties. For when I am weak, then I am strong" (2 Corinthians 12:9-10). Paul didn't run from his weaknesses, he embraced them as an opportunity for God's power to be made evident in his life.

I have learned to lean heavily on this truth that in my weakness, Christ is strong. Through all my struggles and all God was asking me to do that I just couldn't do, I now had a renewed love of this verse.

As I began studying this passage, the part I really liked was the part that says, "My grace is sufficient for you, my power is made perfect in weakness…so that Christ's power may rest on me." That's how I began memorizing this verse, because that was exactly what I needed. After shrinking back for so long, I was ready for God to use me, but was also anxious, fearful, and full of dread. Instead of embracing my weaknesses, I hated them and wanted God to take them away. I could never truly see myself honestly boasting in my weaknesses, and embracing them. Boasting in them, allowing God to use them was the furthest thing from my mind. I'd seen them, recognized them, and wanted them gone. So, I skipped that part of the passage about boasting. I wanted to be the poised, confident, person that I knew I was not. *I wanted to be someone else.*

Before long I felt God say to me, "There's more to those scriptures." See, I thought that if God was calling me to do all these things that I wasn't good at, or afraid of, or that I was too weak for, that He would take away my weaknesses and make me good at those things He was asking me to do. That wasn't what happened. He pointed me back to the verses in Corinthians that I was mumbling through and especially to the part I was skipping over—the part about "…I will boast all the more gladly about my weaknesses so that Christ's power may rest on me. That is why I delight in weaknesses, insults, hardships, persecutions and difficulties, because when I am weak, then I am strong" (2 Corinthians 9b-10).

This brought me to yet another shift of perspective. I had to be able to step out in areas in which I feel weak, untalented, and not good, and allow God's strength to be made perfect in my weakness. I had to learn to obey, even if I feel weak. Even if God asks me to do something that I think I can't do. Even if I don't know how, and it makes me scared. This perspective shift allowed me to step out in obedience and do things I didn't feel confident in or equipped in doing, with no assurance that I would ever develop the confidence or skill I knew was lacking. With no promise that I would get "good at it." There's a big difference between undertaking a task, knowing that even if you aren't good at it from the beginning you will be good at it one day, versus undertaking that task knowing you will repeat the task many times and always feel ill-equipped in the process. That requires complete reliance on God to provide that grace that is sufficient and that strength that is made perfect in weakness.

If we step out to do what we think we're called to do, and do that with the notion that we are one day going to become proficient at that task and won't always stumble through it, we won't need God. But if we undertake a task about which we feel inadequate and we do so with no precondition that the inadequacy will one day evaporate, then we have learned to lean heavily on God. We've acted on what God told us to do with no expectation that we will receive anything in return. That was the challenge for me. Would I do what God said to do—speak in public, lead a Bible study, launch the women's ministry—with no assurance that I would ever magically change into the personality I thought I needed?

As I followed God's leading, what I experienced was exactly what I'd read about Paul's experience. When we step out in weakness, that's when God's strength kicks in. *That's when Christ's power rests on us.* That's the perfect place to be with God—operating in His power and His strength, not our own. Each step I took, God caught me, held me in His hands, and let His strength carry me.

God doesn't want a different you, or a different me. He made each of us, weaknesses and all, just the way He wanted us. When we yield all that we are to Him, weaknesses included, *He takes what we aren't and fills us with what He is.* His call to us is an invitation to surrender everything. Our strengths—which really are no strengths at all—and our weaknesses—which really are no hindrances at all—and delight in how He made us to walk in His Grace and His Power. He won't accomplish His will in our lives by making us different people. Rather, He will empower us to do His will through His grace and strength. He wants us to exchange our weakness for His strength. Then it won't matter if we are weak, because He will be strong in us.

By stepping out in obedience, I learned to delight in my weakness and acknowledge that I needed Him in those weaknesses. I said to Him "I can't, but I know you can. I can't do this in my weakness, but I am thankful for your power that is made perfect in that weakness."

Now, as I said, that was scary for me at first, but what I found was sincere freedom and relief. I didn't have to pretend any longer that I was someone I knew I was not, and I no longer needed to feel burdened about the things I couldn't do. I knew that accomplishing the assigned task was no longer up to me. It was up to God. I was free to be me, and let God move through me. In fact, *I learned to lead from a place of weakness and rest in His ability.*

Most of us want to walk in God's power and grace. Doing that takes willingness on our part to be vulnerable. It takes being obedient even when asked to operate in an area in which we may not be well versed. To do God's will and walk in His purposes we have to step out in faith to do what He has called us to do. That is not always easy. In fact, just taking that first step often seems impossible to do, or the exact opposite of what we want to do or think should be done. Obeying God usually is not convenient either, and rarely fits into our schedule or plan. But delighting in your *weaknesses,* stepping out in your *weakness,* and taking that first step toward the task He has called you to do places you in a position to receive His power in your life.

So, is God asking you to step into an area for which you think you aren't good enough? Are you being called to do something you are scared to do, or that you think someone else could do better? I always think that. I tend to think someone else can do better what God asks me to do. You can't allow yourself to settle for those kinds of fears and thoughts. Welcome your weakness and choose to operate in His strength when you think you can't do it. God doesn't see who you aren't. He sees who you can be. He sees who He made you to be as you yield your weaknesses to Him and receive His power in exchange.

Chapter Seven

# It Takes Effort

*May the favor of the Lord our God rest upon us; establish the work of our hands for us—yes, establish the work of our hands. Psalm 90:17 (NIV)*

The first time I prayed Psalm 90:17 I was stooped over a pile of rocks at the edge of Choctawhatchee Bay near Destin, Florida. That might sound like a desirable place to be for most, but that day as I prayed I was in a place of desperation.

Justin and I were youth pastors—several ministries positions before we planted our current church—and in true Justin fashion, he had decided to launch another grand venture. This time it was creating our own youth camp.

We had attended camps with our youth groups for several years at denominational facilities and somewhere in that experience, Justin found this God-sized dream to create his own camp that combined amazing beach fun and life changing worship services for teenagers. To do that, we needed a location on the beach so Justin started calling facilities in Texas, the closest place to us that was on the coast. None of them was big enough to handle several

44

hundred kids plus their normal summer season. But rather than give up on the idea, Justin worked his way eastward along the Gulf Coast. Through Louisiana, Mississippi, and Alabama he met with the same result—our camp was too large, their facilities too small—until he started calling in Northwest Florida and found the Sandestin Golf and Beach Resort. They had a conference facility large enough for almost any size group we wanted to bring. Justin was ready to do it.

This summer camp idea might not sound like much now but back then it was the biggest thing we'd ever tried to do. As you know by now, all Justin could see was the positive side—the possibilities for spiritual growth and how much fun the experience would be for so many teenagers. I saw only the scary side and was overwhelmed with thoughts like, "People's children could drown, get attacked by a shark, or get horrible sunburn." Not to mention the nightmare of how to keep track of several hundred kids at such a large location. I was scared to death.

As we planned for our first summer, we drove to Florida to meet with the group reservation planners at the resort. After a few meetings, I bowed out and went to look around.

Outside the conference room, I found myself standing in a beautiful courtyard with a pool that overlooked the bay. A wrought iron fence separated the courtyard and pool from a rocky shoreline that faced the bay. It was the middle of the week during their off season and no one was around. So, I slipped through the fence and crouched down on those rocks with water from the bay lapping at my feet.

The details we'd been discussing and the thoughts I'd been thinking about this camp left me overwhelmed, but as I stared across the bay I was amazed by the majesty of God.

The ocean has always reminded me of the power and wonder of God, but that day it also reminded me of how big He is and how small I am.

With the water at my toes, I took a few deep breaths and then began to talk to God about my smallness. About how I married a dreamer and how that was difficult for me because I was always reluctant to take bold risks for Him. I told Him that I would work my guts out to coordinate the rooming lists, create registration packets, conduct parent meetings, train adult leaders, and do all that went into creating and running a youth camp, but that I still knew I would fall short and fail without His blessing, favor, and protection. I asked for all those things from Him to cover our camp. Then I specifically ended by praying the things I'd read in Psalm 90, asking that the favor of the Lord rest upon our newly formed camp and for Him to establish the work of our hands. It was up to us to work as hard as we could, and up to Him to establish that work.

Since then, that has been one of my favorite verses to pray in all of our ministry endeavors, especially planting Foundations Church. Anytime God asks me to do something that I know I cannot accomplish, I draw on those words from Psalm 90 and pray, "…establish the work of our hands."

There are at least two key parts to this scripture. This first is the idea that we must *work*. If God is to establish the work of our hands, we must first be working. We have to put effort into the dreams that God gives us. God uses people to accomplish great tasks and He does it by using our hands, feet, voices, minds, and energy. He expects each of us to move on His behalf, to give all we have, and do our part.

The second key to understanding that scripture is the idea that as we work for God, He establishes that work. In the

Hebrew language, the word establish is *Yacad*. Yacad means to lay the foundation, to fix and to ordain. Webster's defines *establish* as "to cause something to be widely known, to put someone in position for a long time, or create something lasting." That sounds like what most people would want to accomplish in life. We want to create something lasting, to be in a position to have influence in this world, and to see God ordain and fix our work in place. It's not our job to get ourselves into a position of permanence. It's not our job to create something lasting. That is *God's job*. Our job is to work; His job is to establish.

In referencing working for God, I'm not talking earning salvation. That comes from God as a free gift through Christ. You can't earn salvation by doing good works. When I talk about work, I'm talking about what happens after we come to know the Lord, as God fills us with purpose and calling for our lives. It's the kind of work for God that James describes as faith in action. To see that dream fulfilled in our lives that God has put there involves effort and work on our part. Just like it did for Solomon as described in 1 Chronicles 28. David was giving Solomon instructions for life and for building God's Temple. The dream Solomon would undertake was described by David as an enormous work. Therefore, David gave him this charge, "Be strong, and do the work."

Work takes many forms and part of our work is simply the act of doing. When we first started Foundations Church, and met in that school building, volunteers arrived early on Sundays to set up everything we used for the morning worship service. Afterward, they stayed late to take it all down. Justin and I were right there with them, doing the everyday, ordinary things necessary to make the worship service a reality, but those services could not have happened without the help of volunteers who sensed a calling from God to help and then put hands and feet to that calling and got busy working to complete the tasks at hand. If they'd sensed God prompting them to help, but never got off the couch and made the effort to help, the services would have not happened. We have to hear God call us and do what He asks in order to see God's result in our lives.

1 Chronicles 28:9-10 (NLT) also says, "And Solomon, my son, learn to know the God of your ancestors intimately. Worship and serve him with your whole heart and a willing mind. For the Lord sees every heart and knows every plan and thought. If you seek Him, you will find Him. But if you forsake Him, He will reject you forever. So take this seriously. The Lord has chosen you to build a Temple as His sanctuary. Be strong, and do the work."

While Solomon was instructed to be strong and do the work, he was also charged to learn to know God *intimately.* Your work for the Lord might be something like the work we did—traveling to a new city to start something so big you're not sure it'll ever work out. Or it might be organizing events and leading a Bible study. Or doing the everyday tasks necessary to keep your family moving—cooking, cleaning, taking kids to school, or getting to a nine-to-five job. Whatever you do with your time and energy to further the calling you've received from God—that is your work.

And while life today involves a lot of doing—and much of that doing is necessary—sometimes it's easy to get lost in the details of whatever we're trying to accomplish, and forget the effort needed on our part of *being* with God and knowing Him intimately. There's a balance between them both.

Sometimes it is easier for us to do things for God, rather than be with God. It's difficult in our culture to be still in the presence of God, intimately listening, reading, and praying. One way to address that situation is to be disciplined to build in time alone with God, before you set out to do the work of your calling. To set aside time specifically in His presence to listen, read and pray. When we do that, it's much easier to sense His wisdom and guidance in the specific tasks of our calling.

I know this sounds elementary, and very basic, but we get worn out being busy. Our time is limited, and we are pulled in so many directions, it is actually very difficult to have the discipline to implement this into our lives on a daily basis. This idea of reserving time for God each day is counterintuitive to our overly busy, rushed American culture. Our culture tells us that if we aren't so busy that we have ten things too many to do each day then we're lazy. If we aren't burning the candle at both ends and have a do list that is impossible to finish, then we're wasting time. We all have friends who compete to see who's busier and brag about how much they have to do as a way of making themselves feel important. I might even venture to admit that I have done that a time or two. That urge to always be the one doing more can suck us into a life focused solely on the doing, not the being of our life with God.

If we want to make the effort to work for God, we have to be with God every day to find out *how* we are supposed to work for Him—to know what we are supposed to do with our minutes, our hours, and our days. God will direct our path, but we have to let Him, and part of allowing Him to do that requires us to listen. That means, every day, we must meet with God, the creator of the dream that He is establishing. If we don't meet with Him, we won't know what to do. We have to cultivate an intimate relationship with Him so that we know His voice and sense His specific direction for us.

Many of you can recall a time before caller ID was invented. Back when someone called on the phone there wasn't a message on a tiny screen telling us the name and number of the caller. Instead, there was only the caller's voice and as soon as they spoke, we knew who they were—especially with friends and family—because we'd talked to them many times before. Most of the time, none of us bothered to announce our name. We just started talking, relying on the familiarity of our voices to identify us to each other. And it worked. We knew each other's voice because we had talked to each other often, in many different settings, and could recognize each other's voices anywhere, anytime.

That's the familiarity we're supposed to have with God's voice. We are supposed to talk to Him so many times, and on such a consistently regular basis, that we recognize His Voice when He speaks—whether we're praying in the bedroom, walking through the grocery store, or driving down the road.

When we make the effort to connect with our Father, we get to know the heart of God. Knowing His heart—His intention, His desire—gives us direction for our dream. It also gives us sensitivity to the Holy Spirit so that we can hear Him more readily each time He speaks to us.

Psalm 37:23 in the New Living Translation says, "The Lord directs the steps of the Godly. He delights in every detail of their lives. Though they stumble, they will never fall, for the Lord holds them by the hand." Many of us know this scripture in The King James Version as "The steps of a good man are ordered."

Think about how much effort we make each day and all the details of our daily lives. Many times we think the steps that are ordered are only the big steps, like buying a house, going to college, getting married, or taking a job. God wants to order all of our steps—especially the daily ones.

God has a plan for our days but often we miss that plan because we are too busy to consult with Him. Maybe we hear Him on the big decisions, but what about walking daily in power that changes the lives of the people around us? What about walking in God's dream for us every day and not just waiting for that big boom to come to make it happen?

We can see an example in Scripture of the negative consequences of not consulting with God on His Plan. After Moses died, Joshua became the leader of the people of Israel. He was a Godly man and under his guidance, they finally entered the long awaited Promised Land. In their first battle they took the city of Jericho and went on to defeat every enemy in Canaan who came against them. Before long, they were so feared that neighboring kings formed alliances with others in hopes that their combined forces could somehow defeat the army of Israel.

The people of Gibeon, however, tried a different tactic. Rather than confronting Israel on the battlefield, they resorted to deception. They loaded their donkeys with weathered bags, wineskins with old patches on them, while wearing worn out sandals and ragged clothes. They even went to the trouble of drying out their bread to make it appear moldy and crusty so it looked as if they were travelers who were a long way from home, when in actuality, they were neighbors trying not to be overtaken. See Joshua 9:3-6.

Joshua knew that God had said Israel should not enter into treaties with the people of Canaan. As the Gibeonites approached, Joshua asked them who they were and where they were from, but the people of Gibeon lied. They showed him the worn out shoes, which were fakes, and the moldy bread, that they claimed had been in their bags for a long journey. Yet while his checking, and *doing* what he thought was right, Joshua *did not consult with the Lord* and instead "...made a peace treaty with them and guaranteed their safety" (Joshua 9:14 NLT). Three days later Joshua realized the people with whom he'd made the treaty lived nearby and that he had been tricked.

It doesn't matter how close we've been to God in the past, or how much effort we put into the work of our calling, we have to consult with God and spend time with Him each day. Even on our best days, we can't always see the deception the enemy is sending our way. And if we're running solely on emotion or relying on our feelings as a means of discernment, it becomes even more difficult to hear His voice and see His plan. We can't get too busy doing the work that we aren't asking God every day about His Plans. We have to make effort to stay rooted in and connected to God.

God really put this into my heart after we planted a church and began to pastor. As I said before, when we first started Foundations Church I was hiding from what God had for me because I was scared. God had specific daily plans for me that I wasn't realizing. I was doing the big things right, making a daily effort to do things for Him, but I wasn't waking up every day ready to live out the purpose God had for me in the moments of that day. Consequently, there were daily opportunities that I missed.

When God began to reveal that to me, I made an effort to set Him as the priority of my daily life. I know what you're thinking—I am a pastor's wife and I wasn't making God the top priority? For those of us who live in a "Christian bubble"—one where church is at the center of our lives and most of our social interaction involves other Christians—we find it easy to say that God is the number one priority in our lives, but saying it isn't enough. He isn't really first in our lives until we invest in time with Him. Our time is a valuable resource. I believe it's more valuable than money. We have to choose to spend our resource of time with God. I was allowing all the overwhelming circumstances of life, when we first started the church—like two small children at home all day, and all the planning and work to launch a church, to keep me from being with God, and the lack of it was obvious in my life.

Putting God first among the priorities of our daily life and following steps that are ordered by God is not comfortable. It's not *our* way, and it's not always easy. But even though it presents God-sized challenges, it also presents us with the potential to experience the supernatural and miraculous. God has supernatural, uncomfortable, miraculous things for us to do and we often miss those opportunities because we don't consult with Him and let Him order our daily steps. *We want the power of God in our life, but we don't spend that time in His presence that would allow Him to give us that power.* When we spend time with Him, He can change us and empower us to be useful. If we want to walk in power, we need to stay on our knees with Him.

Not too long ago we did a month-long church-wide fast during January in preparation for the upcoming year. Fasting, for most Christians, usually means abstaining from eating or sacrificing an activity for a period of time by replacing it with a time of prayer and renewed focus on God. That year, most of the staff at our church did the Daniel Fast, which means following the dietary plan laid out by Daniel in the Bible. I had done it before but felt like that wasn't the right direction for me that year.

I sensed God leading me to do something different, and I didn't want to just follow along with what everyone was doing. I wanted what God wanted. So, I prayed about it and felt God was asking for more of my time. That was a good general idea, but for it to work as a spiritual discipline I needed to know the specifics of what He meant so I went another step further and asked God what activity I should give up from my daily schedule. He said, "Sleep." He couldn't have picked a more difficult challenge for me.

That may sound weird to you, but I love sleep. I don't give up my sleep without a fight and when I do, I'm grumpy. I am not a night owl or a morning person. I go to bed early and very much dislike getting up in the morning. Over the years, I've even prayed for God to make me a morning person but it hasn't happened. I am a sleeper.

To make things worse, I am a sleeper who doesn't get to sleep much. No one else in our family likes to sleep. My husband has nonstop energy morning, noon, and night without tiring and he's always up for anything. Sleep is not on his radar. He would rather have fun than sleep. Our daughters are the same way. They wake up every morning around six—even on Saturdays and holidays. So, when God asked me to give up sleep I knew I was going to do it, but I was not happy about it.

Begrudgingly, I set the alarm an hour earlier every day for the month of the fast. I won't say I wasn't sleepy because I was, but I will say spending an extra hour with my Father each morning completely transformed my day, my week, and my month. Making the effort to have that connection with Jesus by putting Him first and hearing His voice each morning gave me the grace, strength, and direction every day that I needed. If we want to hear God when He speaks, we have to have a relationship with Him that's close enough for us to hear the sound of His voice and recognize when He speaks. And we have to give God our attention and listen. We can only do that when we spend time with Him.

Our youngest daughter, Chloe, is full of energy and full of life and fun. She often goes in three different directions at once, twirling, singing and chasing. So when I say, "Chloe put your shoes on and brush your teeth," she keeps twirling and singing. She hears the sound of my voice but what I say doesn't really register. And even though I might say it a few more times, she still twirls and giggles. To get her attention, I have to stop her and say, "Look at my eyes Chloe." Once she does, and I say very slowly and clearly, "Please put your shoes on and brush your teeth," she hops up from the floor and does it. In order to get her to obey and do the things I tell her to do, I have to first get her attention.

That's true for us, too. God speaks to us all day long, but much of the time what He says doesn't really register with us. In order to communicate effectively with us, He needs our attention and for that He needs our time. To get that we have to pause in our rushing around. We don't have to be like the rest of the world, running ragged. That's not God's standard anyway. God doesn't ask us to be that busy. He asks us to be still with Him.

Psalm 47:10 out of The Message says, "Step out of the rushing traffic and take a long look at God." You may have memorized that scripture out of the New International Version as "Be still and know that I am God."

Life can feel like rushing traffic. Scripture tells us to step out of that traffic and take a long look at God. It doesn't say wave at God as we zip by in the traffic of life. It doesn't say multi-task and talk to Him while you make school lunches—

although I do that and its okay at times—it just can't be all we do with God. Scripture says instead to step out of the traffic and stop long enough to take a long look at God.

It's when you are alone with God that your steps become ordered and not scattered in different directions. From that, the efforts you make to obey what you've heard from Him are filled with power and purpose. You might think finding your dream with God and having your steps ordered by Him means *doing* more, but it's not about doing more of your own choosing. It's about *being* with Him to hone in your direction. So it's not really about how much you do, but what you do. There's a difference. And when you find that finely honed direction, then He can establish the work of your hands and you can be fruitful for Him. It begins with a specific question each day. That question is simply, "Lord, what do you have for me today?"

When my daughter, Chloe, was four years old she began Pre-kindergarten at our local school. It was half-day pre-kindergarten, which really wasn't half a day at all. It was about three hours long, which only gave me about two hours to get stuff done while she was in school. By the time I dropped her off, went to the gym, and then to the grocery store, it was time to get in line to pick her up. That meant I still had "stuff" to do once I got home with her.

As the year began, I was expecting a typical day to go like this—I would pick up Chloe, have lunch with her, talk about her morning, and play a few minutes with her. Then, she would go about her day playing and leaving me alone while I would get my stuff done. That "stuff" being laundry, dishes, emailing, planning, studying, etc. I don't know why I so naïve as to believe this would happen. I wasn't new to this mom thing. We had two children and I knew how things usually worked out. But that's how I *wanted* it to go.

This is how it really happened—I picked her up and we went home and had lunch, talked and played, then I would politely say, "Chloe, you can go play now and mommy has some work to do." Then she would ask, with enormously cute eyes and such a sweet heart to please, "I want to work with you. Mommy, what do you have for me to do today?" I would try to convince her otherwise, but she insisted on helping me, so we folded laundry together, washed dishes together, and did whatever else I could handle with her by my side.

About every fifteen minutes I would tell her I was done and she could go play, but she wanted to do the next job with me. I was extremely frustrated with this and each day I did everything I could to get her to play by herself and allow me do what I needed to do. But she kept asking, "Mommy, what do you have for me to do today?"

Sometimes I gave her a job to do on her own, thinking she would get distracted from me and I could get things done. But when I gave her a job, she would do it and march right back to me and ask, "Now, what do you have for me to do?" She was relentless.

One day during this process, God stopped me in my tracks and told me to stop trying to change her little mind and embrace the phase that she was in. And He reminded me that this was the last year I would have with her at home—the next year she would be in school all day—so I should enjoy it and stop worrying about all the *stuff* I had to do and just *be* with my little girl.

The second point God made was that the way Chloe came to me was the way I should be coming to Him every day. I should come to Him with open eyes and open ears, asking, "Father, what do you have for me to do today?" I should be just as relentless with God as she was with me.

That's the real *stuff.* Not laundry, email, and studying. Spending time with God, spending time with Chloe. Enjoying the irreplaceable moments with Him and with her. That was the stuff that mattered and when I think about it now it brings tears to my eyes to know that, left to my own devices, I would have traded those moments for laundry, email, and whatever else seemed important.

Be careful to look at your lists and your agendas, then hand it over to God and say, "This is what I have planned today, but what do *You* have for me to do today?" Then take His plan and make it yours with the added prayer, "Don't let me miss out on your ordered steps today."

Ephesians 5:15 in the New International Version says, "Be very careful then how you live, not as the unwise, but as the wise, making the most of every opportunity, because the days are evil." Every moment of our day matters. How we spend our time, who we talk to, what we say. It all matters. God is telling us to be careful with our time and with our opportunities. Don't squander the time by filling it with the busy-ness of a preset agenda. Make the effort to give your time to God. Let Him tell you how to fill it. And He will. God has plans, purposes, and dreams for our lives. He's waiting for us to yield our time to Him, which means yielding our schedules, too.

In the past, I was often afraid to ask God what He wanted me to do because I was afraid He would ask me to do something I couldn't accomplish. Now I say, "Who wants to do something that a human could accomplish anyway?" I want to do something in this world that only God can accomplish. I am so glad He uses imperfect, weak people to accomplish His amazing, God-sized dreams, because that is just who I am—imperfect and weak. And He won't ask us to do anything that He can't accomplish through us. It won't be something we can do on our own, but something He can do with us. We do what we can and then He does what we cannot.

In his book *Circle Maker*, Mark Batterson defines favor as God doing for us that which we cannot do for ourselves. That's God establishing the work of our hands. We find Him doing that as we make the effort to work *for* God and as we develop the discipline of being *with* God while we work.

Chapter Eight

# It Takes Trust

*I am the vine, you are the branches. If a man remains in me and I in him, he will bear much fruit, apart from me you can do nothing. John 15:5 (NIV)*

Trust is an interesting issue. It's much easier to talk about, than apply it to our lives. It's a favorite church topic. We hear about it all the time, and for those of us who grew up in Sunday School, we know we are supposed to say that we completely trust God to meet our needs. But actually doing that—letting go of our particular situation and truly allowing God full control—is quite another matter. Especially in times of deep hurt or overwhelming need, when we want to step in with all our might and "fix" the situation, or drop trust all together and feel like God has forgotten us.

Taking charge and doing things ourselves gives us a sense of control over our circumstances. A false sense, but a self-satisfying one nonetheless. Trusting God feels vulnerable—especially if you want things to turn out *your* way—and not many of us enjoy being placed in vulnerable positions that we can't control. To trust God completely means knowing situations will turn out the way God wants them to, understanding that might be the opposite of what we would choose, and resolving to be okay with that enough to have true peace knowing God will do what is best for us and for His Name.

While yielding to God's control and trusting Him, we sometimes are overwhelmed with such a great need, or so deeply discouraged that what we need God to do for us can't even be put it into words. In those situations, we often find ourselves unable to call out to God and adequately describe our need in words that make sense. It's painfully difficult to put our trust in God in those times.

Like when my daughter, Charli, found out her teacher was diagnosed with cancer. My head was swirling with worries and there were so many things to pray about for her that I couldn't articulate anything with much clarity.

Or when my Papaw had to begin caring for my grandmother, who was diagnosed with Alzheimer's disease. They'd been married, and pastored many churches together, for more than sixty years and she couldn't remember any of it. He was retired from pastoral ministry but still had dreams—to travel and do missions work, to see the world and see lives transformed for God—but none of that was possible with my grandmother's condition. That felt too big for me to begin praying for, and I didn't know how to put the ideas and emotions into words.

And then there was the time when Justin said, "We're starting a church." Just that one statement created enough fear in me that I was too overwhelmed to pray specifically—and that was right when I needed to pray the most. All I could do was ask God to have His way with circumstances that concerned us—issues He knew far better than I did.

When I am in those kinds of situations—overwhelmed with need or discouraged—I often pray a simple prayer I picked up from a book called, *Prayers That Avail Women Much.* The prayer says simply, "God please perfect those things which concern me." When I pray that, it's because there are too many thoughts, worries and feelings to express. That prayer encompasses all of those overwhelmed and jumbled concerns and entrusts them to God. It says to God to conform my circumstances to His will. That's what I ask. It's the same idea we find in the Lord's Prayer when Jesus says, "Your Kingdom come, Your Will be done on Earth as it is in Heaven." We're asking God—whose sovereign will reigns perfectly—to make His will complete in our lives.

When we pray that kind of prayer, we're leaving our lives, our situation, and our needs in God's hands. We are asking Him to interpret the details of our circumstances, and decide the correct course of action for our lives. We're handing Him our very lives and asking for His desire, not our own. That takes a gut level kind of trust. The first time I truly found that gut level trust was when we stepped out to plant our church. When God puts an impossible, God-sized dream in your heart, it will take that kind of trust to allow Him to accomplish that task through you.

Maybe you need that gut level trust to start a business, foster a child, or choose a college. Whatever it is that may be too overwhelming to put into words, that is when to cast all your cares on God and ask Him to perfect those things which concern you, and trust Him. It's in these types of situations and in all situations really, that we have to trust that He hears us, and He will most definitely take care of it according to His plan and His timing.

## Perfectly Weak

When we moved Foundations Church from the school where we first began meeting to the church building a few blocks away, we held a Grand Opening celebration. I found myself very excited and overwhelmed at all God had done to bring us to that day. And not just the things He'd done in the life of the church, but in my own personal life as well.

For the first three years, I had been happy to sit back and let God "do the rest" as He promised to do, and while we were celebrating the grand opening, I realized how miraculously He had done that. He had done everything we had not known how to do, didn't have the money or resources to do, and hadn't even thought of doing. And while He was building the church and establishing it, He'd gently, but insistently, moved me from the back row to the front row and grown me into a participant in His plan.

In celebrating that day, I should have been able to bask in the moment and enjoy all God had done, but I didn't. Instead, I became very aware of how far we still needed to go. Rather than celebrating how far we'd come, I focused on all there was yet to do. In fact, it actually felt like there was more to do then, than there was at the very beginning of starting the church. I began to stress about how we were going to do all the things left undone. There was all this wonderful ministry growing, yet I was focusing on all that needed to be done—all the holes left to fill. I began to panic because we didn't know how to get to the next level and complete what was incomplete. And just like that, I took the burden off of God and put it back onto myself, and the church staff, to accomplish God's vision for the church.

It took a while for me realize what I was doing, and when I put my focus back on God's ability and not my own, He let me know, "I said that if you would be willing, I would do the rest. That doesn't just mean until the church's fourth anniversary and grand opening—that means permanently."

I had stopped trusting momentarily that He would do the "rest," and felt it was up to me, and up to the others around me. That is a difficult balance for us to find. We waiver back and forth between operating in our own efforts and then stepping back and trusting God. We pick up the burdens and we lay them down, only to pick them up again. We just can't quite get the trust issue resolved.

One thing that helps bring balance and perspective to our lives is Scripture. That sounds basic—the spiritual version of eat your veggies—but when the Word of God is an active part of our daily life, it reminds us of His perspective that engenders trust. That makes all the difference. If we have too much confidence or trust in our own thoughts and feelings, we can go our own direction, build our own kingdoms, with God as an after-thought.

When we hold God's Word in our hearts and use scripture daily—it transforms our minds and refocuses us back to the God that we can trust. It reminds us who He is, and how much he loves us. The truth of God's word tells us that He leads us and directs our path. He makes the way when we can't see any way at all. He helps us run the race we are called to with confidence—in Him, not in ourselves.

The balance is that we can't trust in self, and we can't lose confidence in God. Test everything by the Word. Go to God with every question, and every decision to make. Trust His answer.

———

If one side of the trust issue asks the question, "Can we trust God?" the other side asks, "Can God trust us?" If He leads us into the unknown and the supernatural, will we go?

Can He trust us with the lives of others—to bring them to Jesus, to parent them, to love, to give, to be unselfish, and to put their needs before our own? To truly die to self and let Christ rule in our hearts, we won't mind being last so that others can be first. We will be willing to give all the glory to God and take none of it for ourselves? We will be trustworthy—and useable?

Philippians 2:3 says, "Do nothing out of selfish ambition or vein conceit, but in humility consider others better than yourself." We can only be trustworthy to God when we value others more than we value ourselves. When we see them the way God sees them. Our natural tendency is to only see our own needs. It is normal and ordinary to get caught up in pleasing ourselves. When we operate in "self" we put ourselves first. It's only when we operate in the Spirit that we can allow God to produce the extraordinary in us to put others first. The term "dying to self" feels so accurate because I have found it so hard to do. It's a constant inward battle between "what about me" and "what about others."

I want God to be able to look at my life, my words, my actions, and even my thoughts and see no selfish ambition, or vein conceit. As I have thought about that question, I have had to really take time to evaluate several more questions in my own heart. It seems the pull in our culture leads us to make decisions based on self-promotion, and it is easy to get sucked into that world. We can easily fall into the trap of making decisions to further our own agenda, instead of God's agenda. When feelings of jealousy and competition are so rampant, it doesn't always seem expedient to take those thoughts captive and lift others up more than ourselves. We have to search our hearts to discern if God can truly trust our motives—the deep down in our heart motives—which no one else can see.

So, the deeper question to search out is *why do you do what you do?* While you are serving others and God at your church, or in your sphere of influence, it is beneficial to step back and ask yourself, "Why do I do what I do for God?" We can choose to serve to relieve guilt, to meet a membership requirement, for others to see, or because we genuinely love our Savior so much that we will do anything to serve Him and lead others to His life changing, sustaining grace and salvation. It's because of that last reason, we should keep our motives pure and do all we do *just for God*, and to point others to Him, not to ourselves.

As a pastor's wife I'm called upon to do a number of things, and I often think I do a lot for God. Maybe you feel the same way. But sometimes I stop to ask myself, "Is it always *for God*?" Or is it to bring attention to myself? It is to be patted on the back or recognized for all my hard work. It is necessary to stop and gauge our motives from time to time. We are easily swayed by pride, praise and pleasing others. This area of our motives needs continual revisiting in our lives to weigh in different seasons if we are operating solely to please God.

1 Corinthians chapters four tells us that God will reveal our private motives. They are important to God. 1 Thessalonians 2:4 says, "Our purpose is to please God, not people. He alone examines the motives of our hearts." When God examines my heart, I want Him to see that my sole motive in life was to point to Him and to give Him glory, not myself. But that is so hard for us humans. We are so easily distracted by what others think. It is so difficult a task for us to deny self, that I have gone so far as to be excruciatingly honest with God and tell Him that *I want to want to bring*

*Him glory, and not myself. I want to want the praise only directed toward Him. I want to want only His desires and not my own.* My earnest, heartfelt prayer now is, "God, I want to stay so small, so You can be so big in my life. I want to work for You, not for me. I want to build Your Kingdom, and not my own." That prayer echoes John the Baptist's words of, "He must become greater, and I must become less."

Now, there is a way to gain confidence in those tasks we regularly do for God. We can dream with boldness and let God birth visions and goals, and not gain pride. We can work toward greater responsibility and increased competency. We can do all those things, and not do them from a place of pride, if we continually remember that the point of all we do—worship, family life, ministry, everyday jobs—is to lift up the name of Jesus and not ourselves.

Jenni Allen says in her book *Restless,* "We are made to do great things, but we cannot live with motives unchecked. If our motives are for the glory of God, we have tremendous freedom to dream with hearts that are completely His." There *is* tremendous freedom to go after your God-sized dream if your motive is to glorify God. You can feel free to dream big dreams, and pray big prayers, if you are truly seeking heartfelt humility while pointing others to Christ. And there is something to be said about humility these days. Isaiah 66:2 says, "This is the one I esteem, he who is humble and contrite in spirit, and trembles at my Word."

In our culture, it seems as though the right direction would be to make a name for oneself. James 4:10 tells us that if we humble ourselves before the Lord, He will lift us up. Our calling is not to live for ourselves, or a career designed to establish our own position and reputation. We are called to a life of humility that places the interests of others ahead of our own, and to a life of obedience that places God's will above ours. God decides the particular role we play. He is the one who makes our paths straight and accomplishes the dreams He gives us.

It is not our job to lift ourselves up, but it is so hard for us to stay out of that part. It's hard to not be self-promoting, but to be God-promoting. We have to let God do His job with the path of our lives, and let our job be to diligently guard against pride and impure motives, and to guard against selfishness and self-interest.

John says in chapter 15 that apart from Him we can do nothing. We have to remain in God—the vine—to produce anything fruitful at all. A few chapters earlier in John chapter 12, Jesus describes the Pharisees as, "...they loved praise from men more than praise from God." The Pharisees were the religious people of their time. Jesus wasn't talking to the pagans when he gave that description. We have to remember the self-centered traits that seem so obvious in them are also present in our lives, too, because our nature is sinful and selfish. Our very own thoughts and attitudes are self-centered. We naturally think, "what about me?" We naturally compare ourselves with others, and have the inclination to lift ourselves up and step on others in the process. We naturally want to be first, and the best. It's only through the Word of God that we can continually renew our minds and put humility into the forefront of our minds. God's Word reminds us that we are not the focus.

The Old Testament story of Joseph gives us a true example of one who was counted by God as trustworthy. He went from being the baby of the family, who received special treatment as the favorite, to then being thrown into a cistern by his older brothers, sold into slavery, falsely accused of rape, jailed, and left there to be forgotten. But Joseph had a gift of interpreting dreams.

While Joseph was in prison, one of the prisoners he helped was a cupbearer who once had been Pharaoh's servant. Eventually, the cupbearer was released and restored to his position in Pharaoh's household. A few years later, Pharaoh had a dream that troubled him greatly and when he asked for an interpretation, no one could tell him what the dream meant. The cupbearer remembered Joseph and suggested he might be of help to Pharaoh. Finally, after years of mistreatment and being forgotten, God brought Joseph out of jail to interpret the dream.

Having been jailed on false charges, many of us might have refused to cooperate, but not Joseph. If it were up to me, after all those years, I would want to plead my case to Pharaoh. I could imagine, I would have a bad attitude and be focused on defending myself. Joseph, however, prepared himself to be used. He shaved, changed his clothes, and appeared before Pharaoh willing to tell the meaning of the dream. He didn't sulk, or launch into a tirade before Pharaoh about the unjust way he was treated. He simply listened to a description of the dream. Then, with everyone waiting, Pharaoh asked Joseph if he could interpret it.

Joseph easily could have pled his case to Pharaoh about how he didn't deserve the last ten years of his life, or demanded his freedom in exchange for his services. But he did not do that. When Pharaoh called Joseph out of jail and asked for him to interpret the dream, Joseph began his reply with, "I cannot do it."

Joseph led with that sentence. After years of unjust imprisonment, this is his *only* chance, his only way out. And he leads with "I cannot do it." The rest of that scripture in verse 16 says, "I cannot do it," Joseph replies to Pharaoh, "but God will give Pharaoh the answer he desires." He is basically saying, "I can't do it, but God can." He was painfully waiting for the chance to be rescued, and when he gets the chance, he points to God. Not to himself.

In a single moment, Joseph went from slavery and prison to the second most powerful person in the country, second only to Pharaoh himself. Joseph's faith in God and his long suffering allegiance to Him allowed God to raise him up—at the proper time—from prison to the throne.

We have to be at the place in life that we genuinely believe, that attitude of "I know I can't, but God can." That's when you're trustworthy to God. That's when you are usable. That's when He will elevate you.

And when God does elevate you, He will elevate you to save others — as in Joseph's story. When God does speak to you, He will speak to you to reach out to others. When God lifts you up, it's to see others that are lost and hurting. **When God does move through your life, it is still not about you. It's always about you being used for God's glory to save others in so many ways.**

Chapter Nine

# It Takes Overcoming

*For though we live in the world, we do not wage war as the world does. The weapons we fight with are not the weapons of the world. On the contrary, they have the divine power to demolish strongholds. We demolish every argument and every pretension that sets itself up against the knowledge of God, and we take captive every thought and make it obedient to Christ .2 Corinthians 10:3-5 (NIV)*

Heaviness. Pain. Fear. Worry. Doubt. Addiction. Pride. We all have something to overcome. The Bible says we are more than conquerors in Christ Jesus, so why is it so hard to actually *feel* like an overcomer? When the rubber meets the road—or when our feet hit the ground every morning—why can't we seem to change our patterns of behavior or our way of thinking from the things that hinder us to the things that set us free?

Anxiety, worry, and fear have been my biggest struggles. My personality is one that leans toward the shy side anyway, so I have naturally responded by default with fear and worry at times throughout our ministry. That underlying anxiety has ranged from the rather benign reticence to stay home alone at night or aversion to scary movies, to avoiding personal confrontation and risk for God when He calls me. I have been a fairly timid person at times, but it has not *always* been a pervasive and controlling issue in my life.

Surprisingly, once I committed to the dream of planting a church, the grip of fear on my life intensified. When we started Foundations Church, fear and anxiety catapulted into overdrive—and I gave into both. I let them take hold of me, instead of allowing Jesus to take hold of *them*. As a result, they became strongholds in my life. So strong, in fact, that it led to chronic physical pain for several years. And all of this happened as I took courageous steps of faith in the direction of the dream God called me to. When we step out in faith, the enemy fights back. He fights back hard and he fights every step of the way.

Our fifth summer in Tulsa, as we were about to celebrate the fifth anniversary of Foundations church, we had a summer I really loved. Our girls were entering first and third grades that year—and before they left for school— we did our best to squeeze every possible adventure from that time together. They were old enough at that point to have fun with them, and I do love to get every moment I can with my girls as they grow. Each stage is special to me, and I am sad each year they begin a new grade and head back to school.

But as the summer passed and fall approached, fear and anxiety rose within me and the physical pain increased. I was feeling happy and fulfilled in most areas in my life, and I was frustrated with the increasing amount of fear, pain and anxiety that I was feeling. The last couples of weeks that summer were particularly intense, and by then I'd had enough of it and decided that rather than wallowing in all those negative emotions I would fight back. God helped me realize that this struggle was an unwelcomed attack, and that I didn't have to put up with it. It was a battle that I fought frequently, and this time God helped me to respond with an increased intensity of prayer combating this attack like never before.

I've prayed all my life but this time, strengthened by God's word to me, I prayed with a new confidence and boldness. And you can guess what happened next. The harder I prayed, the greater my level of anxiety and pain increased. It seemed the more I prayed and believed things would get better, the worse they became. I would feel this sense of heaviness and dread fall on me like a blanket. I couldn't get out from under it.

Even while this was happening, I still could sense this amazing expectancy that God was moving in my life, my church, my family. I expected good things that fall for our church. I expected blessings that school year for our girls. I knew in my head that God was good and He would bring help in time of need, but my body was hurting, I was fearful, and I couldn't seem to shake it. But I kept praying.

Even when in the midst of seemingly unanswered prayers, it's humbling and amazing to see how God sets up God-moments for you. It's always just when you need Him, and not usually how you see Him coming, but He comes. He reached down into my mess and pulled me so near to Him in the most painful moments I was experiencing. I am thankful for people that were obedient to the voice of the Holy Spirit that helped me and prayed for me, and thankful to my God for being gracious enough save me—even from myself.

So I had (and still have at times) a journey to take to overcome and demolish the stronghold of fear in my life. As I was taken through the "breaking" part of my life over the last fifteen years in ministry, I had not trusted God completely at times, and had withdrawn into fear and worry. I had opened the door to hurt, fear, worry, and relied on those feelings instead of leaning on God. Now I was facing a journey to demolish strongholds.

Over a period of about a year, God led me from scripture to scripture in a process to demolish the stronghold of fear in my life. This process began as I studied and memorized scriptures about spiritual warfare to prepare for a Bible study that I was teaching. The Bible says very clearly that we are at war with Satan and he prowls around seeking whom he can devour. Our enemy wants to kill, steal and destroy us—and not just our dreams but our physical lives as well. Scripture also tells us that we have divine weapons with which to fight against these attacks. I knew this was true and applied to my life in an intellectual sense. I even completed teaching the six-week study about using God's Word to fight this invisible, but very real, spiritual battle we are all engaged in. But as I prepared that study and then taught it for all those weeks, I still didn't realize it was a study to change me as much as anyone else. I had been praying and trying really hard—as if my efforts could create any true change—and I wasn't realizing that God was already moving to change me through studying these scriptures. He was answering my prayers and lifting me out of my mess without me actually seeing it.

That study first focused on 2 Corinthians 10:3-5 (NIV) which says, "For though we live in the world, we do not wage war as the world does. The weapons we fight with are not the weapons of the world. On the contrary, they have the divine power to demolish strongholds. We demolish every argument and every pretension that sets itself up against the knowledge of God, and we take captive every thought and make it obedient to Christ."

I had read this verse many times before, and even memorized it and quoted it as I felt I needed to, but this time I began to dig deeper and researched what the word *demolish* means. As I actively and purposefully focused on demolishing strongholds, God opened my eyes to being truly mindful of the thoughts that I dwell on and how I view strongholds. We aren't powerless against our thoughts, fears, and strongholds—whatever they may be. They can be demolished. Scripture says so. Even though they may seem too powerful to conquer, they aren't insurmountable.

The word demolish in the Greek language that was used in the New Testament means to destroy, to refute, to set free anything bound, to loosen, and to dig under. Those are powerful descriptors of what God is capable of doing in our lives.

I like to go walking and jogging while I pray. I'm sure people notice me and think I'm just talking to myself but I don't care. It clears my mind, rids me of worry and anxiety, and refreshes my soul while I talk to God—so what I look like when I am doing it doesn't really matter. I was in the midst of one of those jogs while studying about strongholds and God gave me a visual example of this "digging under" that He can do to destroy strongholds.

I was telling God I was tired of trying to use my own efforts to get rid of fear in my life—my trying wasn't doing anything anyway—and I needed Him to completely rip this root of fear out of my life. As I prayed that prayer, I saw this image in my mind of a small tree with deep roots. Now, I am no expert gardener, but I do love to make an attempt at gardening each spring and I have learned from experience that it is impossible to uproot a small tree or shrub without the correct tools. I have attempted to uproot them using only my hands, yanking and pulling until my hands were sore, only to find there was no give at all with the roots. I have pulled so hard that I stripped all the leaves off the plant leaving just a wavy, slick stem in the ground, as if mocking my puny efforts. Just like the spiritual strongholds we face in our lives.

Those strongholds that form in our lives often seem small to us but their roots run deep. As I was jogging and praying about this I envisioned that I had pulled and pulled and tried to uproot fear using my own efforts and it hadn't budged. When we get worn out in our own efforts, then it's time to allow God in with His all surpassing greatness and power, to let Him do the work.

God began to show me that over the past few months I had begun to use particular tools to loosen the roots of fear— tools like Scripture and prayer—and how doing that had started to tear down and dig under the stronghold, making me ready for Him to completely reach down and yank that root of fear out. I could actually see the picture in my mind of a shovel loosening a root as a metaphor for the Holy Spirit digging under the root of fear in my life.

That's what the weapons we fight with have the power to do. Satan has no hold on us that Jesus can't dig down to, loosen, destroy or refute. We combat the lies of Satan with the Word of God and the power of His spirit. That's what we use to destroy the strongholds that take root in our lives. Paul wrote in Ephesians about the armor we can use to fight back and defend ourselves See Ephesians 6:10-21. We don't have to allow strongholds to take root. We can choose to be renewed daily in the Word of God.

# Perfectly Weak

When we identify a stronghold in our lives, we often find a big root that is easy to see. However, there are often offshoots of the root that accompany it, similar to the way trees have one big, deep taproot along with numerous smaller ones that branch off. As the Holy Spirit searched my life to rid me of fear, He showed me the big, deep roots that were obvious to me. But God didn't stop there. He began to show me there were residuals of fear that needed to be overcome — like nervousness, worry, dread, insecurity, and doubt. When we allow God access into our lives, He can reveal those things to us, and completely tear down all aspects of the stronghold in our lives.

After God steps in to demolish strongholds in our life, we must be diligent to replace those old ways with God ways. Our daily thought life is a key factor in this. For that, we turn to Scripture using God's Word to protect our hearts and minds when Satan comes against us. If our mind is not focused on God—His plan for us and His particular word to us—it will focus on the surrounding circumstances. I have found that when I am disciplined to yield my mind to the Holy Spirit every day, my mind will not dwell on what I can see or the problems in front of me, but I will focus on what God wants me to see. The scripture I pray to direct my thoughts each day is Romans 8:6 which says, "The mind controlled by the Spirit is life and peace."

This is such a simple scripture. It's not complicated or difficult to understand. Applying it, however, takes a daily commitment to exercise the discipline of yielding our thoughts to the control of the Holy Spirit. Trading our fear, our worry, our anger, our confusion for His life and peace. The commitment to using Scripture in this way enables us to resist the strongholds that Satan tries to build in our lives.

We can literally trade our struggles for God's peace. We can choose what we think on—to have a mind controlled by the Spirit or a mind controlled by the sinful nature. That's why Philippians 4:8 tells us to think on things that are praiseworthy and excellent. Doing that allows the Word of God to renew our minds.

God frequently reminds me of how childlike our faith should be, especially in the area of overcoming attacks and obstacles that come against us. He shows me that lesson most often when I am with my children.

Not long ago we watched the movie, *Rise of the Guardians*. In that film, Pitch Black, a spooky figure cloaked in black, attacks the minds of the children, using fear to steal their belief. In place of dreams and hope he gives them nightmares that cripple their imagination, which causes them a life of constant fear and dread. Hope vanishes and they spend every waking hour expecting the worst.

In the movie, childhoods characters—Jack Frost, the Easter Bunny, and the Tooth Fairy—come alive and help the children remember and recover their true identity. Remembering who they really are opens their minds to the realization that they can choose not to give into the fear. And in the end, they banish Pitch Black simply by saying, "I can see you. I know you are there, but I am not afraid of you."

That's how we should be. We have the power to say the same thing to attacks that come against, to strongholds, and to the enemy who wants to steal our dreams, life, and joy. Not that trouble isn't really there, or that we can't see and feel the battle—those things actually exist and we feel them all the time—but the key is that we don't operate by what we see. We don't give into them because we know that God is greater than any fear we face or stronghold that arises. We know we are in a fight and the dark forces exist, but we don't have to be afraid of them. Jesus has overcome them all.

And just for all you warriors out there, those of you that are reading this thinking, "I am not afraid!" It's not just about being scared. Fear shows up as insecurity, anxiety, doubt, worry, dread, stress, mistrust, nervousness, timidity, or any of the other labels we use to express the uneasiness that comes over us when we doubt God is bigger than our obstacles. If you struggle in any of those areas, you are struggling with fear that's trying to take you out.

Think about how many times we avoid doing what God whispers to us to do because of one of those feelings. So many times we shy away from bold obedience because of what someone else might think of us, or because we think someone else could do it better. Think of how many times you were supposed to say something to someone and didn't because you were nervous or afraid of rejection. There have been many times I have awakened in the morning and decided not to follow through with what I had planned to do that day solely because I was dreading doing it. There are many variations of fear that Satan slips by us and we don't even recognize it, and it keeps us from being effective for the Kingdom of God and living God's dream for our lives.

Recently, God showed me a picture of how I was allowing myself to be hindered, ineffective and not fulfilling my God-given purposes due to fear. It was a silly illustration in one respect, but it got the point across to me very clearly.

Our little dog, Max, is a Westiepoo, which is half West Highland Terrier and half poodle. (Justin cringes every time he has to say the name "Westiepoo" to describe his dog, as if the sound of it threatens his man-card.) Max is a cute little dog and spends most of his time inside, playing and growling and rolling around on the floor. He runs and chases and is the perfect dog for our girls, patiently going along as they dress him in princess clothes and push him around in a stroller.

However, Max is also an extremely skittish dog. He jumps and shakes with fear at the sound of a trash bag, runs and hides anytime the girls and Justin wrestle, and when the Nerf guns come out he heads for the bedroom. He is especially fearful when storms come up and it thunders or in the summertime when fireworks come out. At the sound of it, he trembles and whimpers and refuses to go outside. Even when he needs to go, he won't.

He ought to be outside—he *wants* to be outside— running and barking like a dog should, but just can't. And when he finally can stand it no more and *has* to go out, he bolts from the door into the yard real fast, looks quickly all around for danger, does his business, and flees for his life back into the house as if a monster were chasing him.

Sometimes we watch this process and laugh, because it's really funny to see. The last time, however, I felt badly for him. I was thinking, "He is a dog. He was created by God to live outside. He is supposed to love it out there…chasing, sniffing, and barking, he just can't do what he was made to do. He's been conditioned to be afraid." As I was thinking that exact thought about Max, God said to me, "That's the way I feel about you Casey."

My heart just sank. God used that quirky dog to reveal to me how fear was controlling me. It has for a long time and at many different levels of my life. Just like that dog, I had been created for a purpose but was unable to be what God was calling me to be because I was afraid.

That's when I began to force myself to allow Him to change me. As He showed me that one illustration, it shed so much light on what I was allowing to hold me back in my life. I realized that as silly as Max was to run for his life in the backyard, I was being just as ridiculous. I had the God of the universe on my side, with limitless power, and I was running scared. My natural mindset has always been to worry and to gauge my actions by "what will people think." Now, to allow God to change me, I have to be purposefully disciplined and yield my mind every day to the Holy Spirit, **so I can stop worrying about what other people think, and focus on what *God* thinks about me.** I have learned to pour over the scriptures, write them down, memorize them and quote them when fear tries to creep in. Not as a magic phrase, but to remind myself and remind the enemy who God is, and what He has said He will do. I have decided not to allow fear to hold me back, but to conquer it through the power of Jesus Christ. You can make that decision for yourself, too.

Chapter Ten

# It Takes Transformation

*Do not conform to the pattern of this world, but be transformed by the renewing of your mind. Romans 12:2 (NIV)*

During the first ten years of our marriage, as we served as youth pastors, I often taught the high school Sunday School class. I taught them to memorize scriptures like Jeremiah 29:11 (NIV), "'For I know the plans I have for you,' declares the Lord, 'plans to proper you and not to harm you, plans to give you hope and a future,'" and they learned about Joseph and how God took what Satan meant for evil and turned it around for good. I taught them that God's plans for their lives were so much greater than the plans they could ever make, trying my best to get them to see that God could do far above all they could ask or imagine. I truly believed it for them and wanted those teenagers to plant God's promises deep in their hearts—to pursue God with all their might, and what He had prepared specifically for them. But while I was telling them those things and believing it for *them*, I doubted it for myself. I didn't fully, always, and completely believe it for me.

# Perfectly Weak

Sometimes as I was teaching, fleeting thoughts passed through my mind that I wasn't seeing in my own life the things I was teaching them in class. My life didn't seem extraordinary and I certainly didn't see myself as someone who could do all things through Christ. Instead, I saw the path God had called me to as one that was too hard and too lonely. Rather than seeing God as one who provided exceedingly and abundantly more than I could ask or imagine, I saw only the lack and difficulties we endured.

As I mentioned before, in those early years of ministry my mind was not controlled by the Holy Spirit. I didn't operate in life and peace. I wasn't allowing the Holy Spirit to renew my mind every day through God's Word. It wasn't until I yielded to Him, and daily renewed my mind with God's Word that He changed me, and helped me to believe the promises of God were personally for me. As we grow in our Christian walk, and in our faith, the key is to continually allow God access to change our hearts, our minds, and our perspective.

After God confronted the obvious strongholds in my life, He led me into a transformative process that took on the habits and old thought-patterns that allowed those strongholds to form in the first place. Allowing God in to demolish those strongholds gave Him access to me at a deeper level in my life, and it also motivated me to find the discipline to continually walk in freedom and prevent new strongholds from forming. That transformative process taught me new ways of thinking designed to keep me from returning to old habits and former ways of thinking. This process follows the instructions in Ephesians 4:22-24 which guides us to put off our old self that is corrupted and to be made new in the attitude of our minds and put on our new self.

This road to change was not a straight path for me, but one that was full of twists and turns. It wasn't a quick journey from before to after, but gradual and progressive—though there were several key breakthrough moments. And it wasn't a one-sided process, either. It was part God and part conscious decision on my part—He acted, I chose to respond. It's a life long journey I am still in, away from whom we are in our own nature, striving toward who we can be in Christ.

As we served in various locations in the first ten years of ministry, we definitely had many twists and turns. What began as a very naïve dive into the dreamy world of changing lives, very quickly turned into a harsh reality, which resulted in me turning inward and wondering if God really would ever answer my prayers.

Our first church was our beginning in the transformation process with God. He did call us to vocational ministry, but he never promised it was going to be easy, though we just assumed it would. He did promise to walk us through it. And as he has allowed painful experiences, He has indeed walked us through these events growing our character, our dependence on him, and our humility so that we can be more fully used to bring Him glory. Reminding us that it's never really about us, and always about pointing to Him.

The painful growing times are much like sandpaper in our lives smoothing off our rough edges. When you walk through painful experiences and turn to God, instead of turning away, you are able to live out the scriptures that describe how God refines us in the fire of affliction. Years of these kinds of experiences developed perseverance in my life just as Romans 5:3-4 (NIV) says, "We also glory in our sufferings, because we know that suffering produces perseverance; perseverance produces character, and character, hope."

Fast forward to our last youth pastor position—eight years into ministry. By this point I was definitely feeling "tired of growing." I was in the longest spiritually dry season of my life. We had just left a church where we had felt hurt and moved again. Moving, all by itself is so hard. It leaves you feeling all alone, missing the people you'd just spent years giving your entire life to, and trying to connect to new people that you know you will probably leave again. Plus, I had a two-year-old and a baby. I felt isolated in this season. I felt alone. And at this point, we were also extremely broke financially. I was feeling empty because it was the longest time I had not "felt" the presence of God or "heard" his voice. He was silent.

This period of silence between God and I felt so much to me like the psalmist explained in Psalm 22:1-2 (NLT), "My God, My God, why have you abandoned me? Why are you so far away when I groan for help? Every day I call to you, my God, and you do not answer. Every night I lift my voice, but I find no relief."

I remember so clearly sitting out on our back porch one afternoon during this time while both girls were napping. I was empty, and desperate to hear Him. We had a big backyard with lots of mature trees, which made for a beautiful setting. I stared up at the biggest treetop that met the clouds begging for God to respond to me. I knew He existed. I knew He called me. I knew He loved me, but I just didn't feel it anymore. I was beginning to wonder if I would ever feel it again. I told God that afternoon that even if I never felt Him again, or He never answered any prayers, that I would still love Him and still choose to serve Him. I remember how hard that was for me, and resigned myself to this being a real possibility.

I didn't know it at the time, but that was one of those deep, stretching, and transformational periods of my life. This process was the two years before our venture into church planting. It was part of the breaking process I needed to endure to grow. Those growing times were difficult for me to detect while in the middle of them. My perspective during those times was definitely not on what God was doing in me, but on circumstances happening around me. I can look back now and see the stretching and transformation.

After we had moved to Tulsa to plant the church, one pivotal moment came that I could feel and see, came as I was sitting in my car waiting for a dentist appointment. I had about thirty minutes to wait and I was using the time to listen to worship music and pray. We were about two years into our church plant and I still was holding onto so much fear, hiding from the change God was trying to bring into my life, and struggling to forgive the hurt we had experienced. As I sat there in the car, I began to sob. As I poured my heart out to the Lord, I began to write it all down. This is an excerpt from my journal showing what I said....

*I am afraid of people. I have been deeply hurt. More than once. By so many people. Now I am afraid. Now I don't trust. At all.*

*I am ready God. I want to be changed. I don't want to be like this. Healing is only in your hands. I want to be different. I don't want to be scared all the time anymore. I want to be who You want me to be. I want to be used how You want me to be used. Not held captive by fear.*

*I don't know how. I can't do it. Do it for me, Jesus. I am willing, please do it all for me.*

# Perfectly Weak

Then I wrote what I heard God say to me...

*I allowed it all to happen. I saw it all. I broke you into pieces to fit you back together. This is the last piece I need. The fear. And it's the biggest. You gave it to me, and now I will put you back together whole. I will help you. Just be in my presence. Just look to me. Who cares what other people think. Be you, because I made you exactly the way I wanted you to be. You are the perfect you. I need you to be you because I want to use you. And I can. You can because I can. I am your confidence.*

I know God was moving in me before that moment, but this is when my eyes were opened to the growth that needed to take place in my life. This is when I began to see, feel, and hear the need that existed in my own spirit.

Everything I went through—every heartache, loss, difficulty—all lead to the brokenness, pain, and surrender that are essential to deep lasting growth. And growth hurts. But it is the kind of pain that changes us into the person God wants us to be. He develops the fruit of the Spirit in us—during those growth periods in our life. He is growing us into the person that can be more fully trusted. More fully used.

Don't get me wrong, I have told God on more than one occasion that I was tired of "growing," because it's hard and I didn't want to struggle anymore. Times when it felt like those growing moments came back to back and were never ending.

Now, on *this* side of the experience, I can see that those times were purposeful. God was fulfilling His Plan in me. I didn't like the process but I really wanted the result. I had to learn to allow myself to be transformed, even when it came through difficult circumstances. There was no other way to become a person who could live out the purposes God had planned for me.

We all have to come to a place of surrendering our dreams, our wishes, our personalities, our mindset, and our control to His dreams, His wishes, and His design. We allow God to change us for the goal of operating in His mindset. To begin to daily renew your mind, and operate in that Christ like mindset, you begin to have a perspective shift. We begin to see our circumstances, good and bad, as God moving in our lives and growing us.

Not long ago we took our family on a ski trip for Spring Break. Our kids had never seen the mountains and we were excited to show them. As we approached Denver, Justin and I challenged each other to a contest to see who could spot the mountains first. We looked and looked, squinting over the dashboard into the horizon for what seemed like forever. It took longer than we thought but finally we spotted a line of mountains forming hazy silhouettes against the sky in the far distance.

Once we could see them in front of us the contest was over and we began to argue about who saw the mountains first. In the midst of our friendly argument, we glanced away from the windshield and realized there were mountains on either side of the highway much closer than the ones we'd been staring at in front of us. They were much closer to us and easier to see, but we had been so focused on looking out the front windshield that we completely missed the ones just to the right and the left of us. They were right there all along. All we had to do was turn our heads to the right or left to see something new.

Transformation is a lot like that. Sometimes we need to change our view. Change our perspective. See our circumstances the way God does. Look at things a different way—God's way— to allow transformation to take place in our minds. We won't always understand why God is taking us through a certain valley or along a particular path. Sometimes we have to ask God to help us look at things differently, walk away, or climb the hill to see what we need to see. When we are looking down, looking at things through our human eyes, we need to look up and see things through a Biblical perspective. We need to weigh what we see with what God's Word says about it and with what God is telling us.

----

Throughout this book I have mentioned a number of scriptures and I've done that because throughout my life— and most recently when we moved to start the church—I have found digging into God's Word to be a vital part of allowing God to control my perspective and attitude. And not just to control it, but to shape and conform my mindset to reflect the character qualities evident in His Holy Spirit—love, joy, peace, patience, kindness, goodness, gentleness, faithfulness and self-control. Without scripture to keep me focused on what God wants, I would not have made it through the challenges we faced.

Here are some scriptures I turn to for help. I have memorized most of them and meditated on all of them as a way of allowing God to change my mind and transform my life. Meditating on God's Word has changed me and these are life to me.

2 Timothy 1:7 (NKJV)
"For God has not given me a spirit of fear, but of power, love and a sound mind."

Deuteronomy 30:19 (NIV)
"I set before you life and death, blessing and cursing; CHOOSE LIFE so that you and your descendants may live."

Proverbs 23:7 (NKJV)
"As a man thinks in his heart, so is he."

2 Corinthians 10:4-5 (NIV)
"The weapons we fight with are not weapons of this world——they have divine power to demolish strongholds. We demolish every argument that sets itself up against the knowledge of Christ and take captive every thought and make it obedient to Christ."

John 15:4-5 (NIV)
"Remain in me and I will remain in you. No branch can bear fruit by itself; it must remain in the vine. Neither can you bear fruit unless you remain in me. I am the vine, you are the branches. If a man remains in me and I in you, you will bear much fruit. Apart from me you can do nothing."

Philippians 4:4-13 (NIV)
"Rejoice in the Lord always. I will say it again: Rejoice! Let your gentleness be evident to all. The Lord is near. Do not be anxious about anything, but in every situation, by prayer and petition, with thanksgiving, present your requests to God. And the peace of God, which transcends all understanding, will guard your hearts and your

minds in Christ Jesus. Finally, brothers and sisters, whatever is true, whatever is noble, whatever is right, whatever is pure, whatever is lovely, whatever is admirable—if anything is excellent or praiseworthy—think about such things. Whatever you have learned or received or heard from me, or seen in me—put it into practice. And the God of peace will be with you. I rejoiced greatly in the Lord that at last you renewed your concern for me. Indeed, you were concerned, but you had no opportunity to show it. I am not saying this because I am in need, for I have learned to be content whatever the circumstances. I know what it is to be in need, and I know what it is to have plenty. I have learned the secret of being content in any and every situation, whether well fed or hungry, whether living in plenty or in want. I can do all this through him who gives me strength.

Ephesians 3:16-21 (NIV)

"I pray that out of his glorious riches he may strengthen you with power through his Spirit in your inner being, so that Christ may dwell in your hearts through faith. And I pray that you, being rooted and established in love, may have power, together with all the Lord's holy people, to grasp how wide and long and high and deep is the love of Christ, and to know this love that surpasses knowledge—that you may be filled to the measure of all the fullness of God. Now to him who is able to do immeasurably more than all we ask or imagine, according to his power that is at work within us, to him be glory in the church and in Christ Jesus throughout all generations, for ever and ever! Amen."

Galatians 5:22-23 (NIV)

"But the fruit of the Spirit is love, joy, peace, patience, kindness, goodness, gentleness, faithfulness, and self-control."

John 3:30 (NIV)

"He must become greater; I must become less."

The Word of God holds tremendous transformative power in our lives. Whatever you are facing and however you may need to change, the Bible has the answer. It has guidance, power, wisdom, comfort, direction, hope, healing, restoration, and transformation. Use it. Memorize it. Mediate on it every day.

Put God's Word into your mind and before your eyes as often as you can throughout your day. I have Scripture verses on my computer, on sticky notes on the refrigerator and the bathroom mirror. I have sticky notes on the dash of the car and non-sticky ones in my purse. And every time I see them I'm reminded of God's promises to me, His work in my life, the goals He has set for me. Then I pray the particular scriptures aloud and declare them over my circumstances.

These are the scriptures specific to my journey, to my change and healing God has worked and is working in me. I offer them as an example of how I have searched out the scriptures I needed. You must do the same. Use some of these, or don't, but ask God for the exact scriptures *you need* for the changes He is working in you. Then plaster those words all over your house, memorize them and constantly bring them into your mind daily as you struggle, and as you work to align yourself with the things He is doing in your life.

Chapter Eleven

# It Takes Walking in Power

As a pastor's wife I have often been thrust into leadership positions simply by the fact that I'm the pastor's wife. I have asked God many times, "Why was I chosen to be a leader?" I don't feel like my personality matches with that of a good leader. Justin is so outgoing, thinks fast on his feet, and is naturally a people person. To me, that sounds like the personality of a good leader and I have never felt that description fits me.

So, I am a leader that doesn't feel like a leader. In my mind, leaders are supposed to be confident, assertive, and command attention. More often than not, I feel timid and defeated. I have the tendency to withdraw, hide and hesitate to step out when God asks me to. I have been way less bold due to my tongue getting tied, my mind going blank, and my heart beating out of chest. I have found myself being a "shrinker backer" rather than being bold.

In all of that, I have come to the conclusion that I am in this position for one reason—because God placed me here. That may sound arrogant. I don't mean it that way. God puts each of us where we are in our station—in our calling in life to do what He needs us to do for His purposes.

Once I came to understand that I'm in my place because God wanted me there, my next question was, "Why would I be afraid of what God has planned for me to do?" I have asked myself that question many times, frustrated with how I was feeling. "Why am I afraid to do what God has called me to do, empowered me to do, and equipped me to do?" I know God's Spirit lives inside me and I have all I need to accomplish the things He has asked me to do. So, why do I feel like the tasks He asks me to do are insurmountable? Why do I shrink back in fear? Why am I timid?

The word timid is defined in the *Merriam-Webster Dictionary* as "lacking in courage, lacking in self-confidence." Synonyms include mousy, shy, hesitant, and nervous. Timid also means to fear. Yep, that describes me. There are way too many occasions in which I have found myself lacking self-confidence, feeling mousy, and easily alarmed. It takes just one text message, one thought, one person who is upset with me, and I spiral downward into fear, disease, and nervous worrying. But the Word says *I have not been given a spirit of fear or timidity.*

2 Timothy 1:7, "For God did not give us a spirit of timidity, but of power, of love, and of sound mind." In the Greek language, in which this Scripture was written, timid means fearfulness, cowardice, to shrink back, to retreat, hesitate, to withdraw, to be unwilling due to fear. I have decided that I don't want to live my life in retreat anymore. God has not given me a spirit that retreats, runs away, and hides in cowardice.

So, if God has given me a spirit of power and confidence, where does this sense of timidity and fear come from? If it's not what God intended for me to have, then I can tell it to go, in the Name of Jesus, and it does not control me.

It has no place in my mind or my life. It is an unwelcome spirit of fear and timidity and I can command it to go under the authority of Jesus. So can you.

Spiritual warfare is real. There is a daily battle in our world against our minds, our marriages, our actions, our thoughts, our words, our feelings—our everything. The only way to come against this battle is with God's Word and power of His Holy Spirit. You can begin to protect yourself in this battle by reminding yourself that you have been given the Armor of God. So put it on and take your stand in this fight.

Ephesians 6:10-17 (NIV) says, "Be strong in the Lord and His Mighty Power. Put on the full armor of God so that you can take your stand against the devil's schemes. For our struggle is not against flesh and blood, but against rulers, against authorities, against powers of this dark world and against the spiritual forces of evil in the heavenly realms. Therefore put on the full armor of God so that when the day of evil comes, you may be able to stand your ground. Stand firm then, with the belt of truth buckled around your waist, the breastplate of righteousness in place, and with your feet fitted with the readiness that comes with the gospel of peace. In addition, take up the shield of faith, which you can extinguish the all the flaming arrows of the evil one. Take the helmet of salvation and the sword of the spirit, which is the word of God."

This passage of scripture tells us there are schemes against us and there are flaming arrows aimed in our direction. We aren't told this to scare us, but to remind us that the battle is real and to show us that God has enabled us to stand our ground—a command that is repeated twice in that section of Ephesians—using the armor that He has provided. We have the authority to do that. In fact, the battle has already been won through Jesus. Otherwise, the Bible would tell us to run for our lives. But it doesn't. It shows us that if we prepare ourselves by allowing God to equip us with His spiritual weapons, we can stand against the powers that attack and oppose us.

In her book "Women at War," Jan Greenwood points out the importance of recognizing who our enemy really is. As long as Satan has us deceived about who our enemy is—or we are even oblivious to the fact that we are engaged in a war at all—we can't fight against him. Once we identify our enemy as Satan, not our feelings, each other, or our spouse—then we can resist the enemy in Jesus' name and he will flee.

1 Peter 5:8 says, "Be self-controlled and alert. Your enemy prowls around like a roaring lion looking for someone to devour. Resist him, standing firm in faith." The Amplified Bible says to *resist the devil at the onset.*

I often listen to Joyce Meyer's radio podcasts and in one of those messages she pointed out that that we should resist the devil at the onset, when he first shows up. Not waiting until later, after we've entertained the thoughts and ideas he's tempted us with and are submerged in the muck of a spiritual onslaught. Instead, *resist the devil at the onset.* That's how we stop ourselves from spiraling out of control into the thoughts that Satan wants to use to hinder God's plan in our lives. We are in control of stopping any attack at the onset.

When you feel like you are being attacked—you sense fear coming on, you begin to doubt God's work in your life, or you have a bad attitude, or a fight with your spouse—ask the Holy Spirit to show you when you are being attacked. Ask God to show you when you are no longer thinking the right way, when you're giving into emotions, or when you're reacting the way the enemy wants you to react. Ask God to help you resist these kinds of thoughts and actions and work to identify them when they first appear.

When something happens that throws me into worry—someone hurts my feelings, I have a disagreement with someone, or something happens with my children—my natural reaction is to dwell on it. My mind just plays it over and over and then I get more and more worked up. If I am not in God's Word like I should be, and not yielding my mind to the control of the Holy Spirit, I focus totally on the problem. I will play the "what ifs" in my mind—meditating on the worry and imagining the worst, rather than meditating on Scripture. And as a result, I spiral deeper and deeper into negativity about my circumstance.

Over the past few years as I have focused on yielding my mind to the Holy Spirit, I have learned when I begin to fall into this pattern of thinking, to stop and resist this attack. I've learned to ask God to help me recognize when I start this spiral and resist it from the very beginning.

Satan is stealthy and he goes for our most vulnerable spots, sometimes in ways we don't even recognize as attacks. He goes for the places we refuse to yield to God or the emotional wounds we've received. There is power in realizing in what ways we are most vulnerable.

My most vulnerable spots are fear and worry related. The easiest target for Satan to snag me is worrying about our children. Just one small thought and I'm headed down the road of irrational worrying. It is such a familiar path, that even now I don't always notice it right away. I have to be purposefully disciplined to ask the Holy Spirit to help me recognize attacks like that and resist them.

2 Corinthians 10:5 (NIV) says, "We demolish arguments and every pretension that sets itself up against the knowledge

of God, and we take captive every thought to make it obedient to Christ."

By instructing us to take our thoughts captive and make them obey Christ, scripture is telling us that every thought *can* be made obedient to Him. No thought is beyond His grasp. And He has given us the power—His power—to do that very thing. We can take any thought that comes through our mind and command it to be obedient to Christ, through His power. Christ is already victorious over our thoughts; we just have to give him control of them.

There is great freedom and power in our thought life when we put that verse into practice. When we do that, we realize that we don't have to dwell on every thought that comes into our minds. Satan will try to plant thoughts and lies in our minds that he knows will derail us. He knows our weak spots and what sets us off track. We have to know the Holy Spirit's promptings then, to resist the enemy's lies. That enables us to take authority over those attacks in Jesus' Name, and to choose to not give power to every thought that comes into our minds.

Our thought life is so important to God that He not only gives us instructions to take our thoughts captive—telling us what *not* to think about—that He also gives us directions on what we *should* be thinking about. Philippians 4:6-8 tells us, "Do not be anxious about anything, but in every situation, by prayer and petition, with thanksgiving, present your requests to God. And the peace of God, which transcends all understanding, will guard your hearts and your minds in Christ Jesus. Finally, brothers and sisters, whatever is true, whatever is noble, whatever is right, whatever is pure, whatever is lovely, whatever is admirable—if anything is excellent or praiseworthy—think about such things."

# Perfectly Weak

I love that God doesn't just tell us what not to think about, but leads us into right thinking. When I am spiraling down into worry, I'm not thinking on the praiseworthy and excellent. I'm thinking the opposite. And often I repeat the same cycle of worry, fear, repentance over and over again. Many of the battles we fight repeatedly could be stifled if we focused on the things God has told us to think about.

It's when we are thankful and present our requests to God then peace that transcends all understanding will guard our hearts and minds. When I used to read this scripture I would feel condemned. I would read the part that says don't be anxious and immediately feel defeated. Since I have always been anxious, I felt guilty right off the bat and couldn't get to the part that promises the peace.

Recently as I studied this scripture and meditated on it, I was drawn to that part about immeasurable peace. I focused on the word "guard," and imagined an actual guard at the door of my mind—a giant angel with a sword—checking everything that came in. I know that might sound silly, but it was very comforting to me. After that, I started focusing less on feeling guilty that I do get anxious, and more on the promise of that verse—that the peace of God will guard our minds. If we follow his instruction to be thankful and pray about everything, He will be our guard.

And I offer one final illustration of how subtle and deceitful the enemy's attacks can be. Through the process of studying and seeking God for transformation in my own life, God reminded me of something interesting. As I had been struggling with overcoming anxiety, gripping fear, and paralyzing timidity, one day it very randomly came to my mind what my name means. I knew when I was a little girl what it meant, and I didn't like it, but I had completely forgotten about that.

I have always disliked my name. When I was growing up, Casey was a name most often given to boys and associated with men—like Casey the baseball player of "Casey at the Bat," Casey Jones, the real live railroad engineer. Casey Kasem, a radio announcer many of you will remember. People often referred to me as one of these men when I was a little girl. You can imagine why I didn't like that so well.

On top of that, my maiden name was Boyd, which easily morphed into the word "boy." A first grade classmate named David noticed the nuance of both names and started calling me "Casey Boy." I fought back by calling him "David Girl," but it never had the same impact on him as his name-calling did on me.

My dislike for my first name centered mostly on the fact that I thought it was boyish. It wasn't flowery or beautiful like the names of most of the other girls in class. So much so, that even though I knew the meaning of my name, I still hated it, and even hated it all the more *because* of its meaning. However, there is incredible significance of the meaning of my name now, considering all that I have struggled with.

My name—Casey—actually means "brave." Before I was born, my parents named me "The Brave One." I was stunned when that memory came back to me. I had to let that sink in, in light of all I had been through over the years of ministry and starting our church. I had shrunk back to a place and felt like the mousiest, littlest, most insignificant, fearful and timid person on Earth. And as I clawed and fought my way out of that hole, and refused to let Satan put that on me through God's grace, it was significant for me to remember what I had completely forgotten about my name.

# Perfectly Weak

And as I remembered, God began to speak something into my heart. He knew I was going to be named that. He spoke it to my parents. He knew I would have a quieter, behind-the-scenes-type personality. He knew I would shrink back in fear after being hurt. He knew I would hide. He also knew I would scratch and claw my way out of that hole and respond to His voice. In Bravery. In His Strength, with His Sufficient Grace. As I look back on it all so far, I can acknowledge where I have been brave, stepping out over and over out of my comfort zone and taking risks for Him. I don't *feel* brave when I do these things, but I can see how I am. I am thankful God didn't leave me in my fear and timidity, but lifted me out with His Grace and His Power that rests on me. He has allowed me now, not to stay in the place of being a leader that doesn't feel like a leader, but to move into walking in His strength to be comfortable in my calling and in being me.

Chapter Twelve

# It Takes Dreaming

*Now to Him who is able to do immeasurably more than all we ask or imagine, according to His work within us, be the glory in the church and in Christ Jesus throughout all generations. Ephesians 3:20-21 (NIV)*

Even after traversing down the road of transformation and hurt that God used for my good, I am still not a dreamer by nature. But God is. God has dreams way beyond what I could ask or imagine for my life. There was a time in my life that couldn't allow myself to dream. I had gotten to the point where I was stuck and couldn't believe that even God had a dream for my life any more. I knew He had a plan, but didn't compare that plan to a dream. I had spent so much time operating in my own strength and realizing I couldn't accomplish much, and I just couldn't get past my own self to dream.

This became a pattern very early on in our marriage, as we experienced some difficulties because of my fear of dreaming. Right as we got married, and while we were youth pastors, Justin was always chasing God-sized dreams. He is a man of great vision and passion to see lost people saved.

Consequently, he was always coming up with huge ideas that are fun, exciting, and designed to reach people. As I was learning to be his wife, and youth pastor alongside him, I responded to his dreaming by caving in to the fear. Every time he would share an idea with me, I would tell him how it wouldn't work and what was wrong with the idea. This became the pattern. He would want to do something really big, and I would only want to keep it small and manageable.

After a while, he finally came to me and told me that every time he had an idea that I would shoot it down. I was being his dream-killer. When he said that, I realized it was true. I didn't even see that was what I was doing until he pointed it out. My natural reaction was critical and negative due to fear of what *could* go wrong. I couldn't see the limitless power of God in Justin's vision. I could only focus on what I could see, which was my limited ability.

I had to make a change. I needed to adjust my perspective and attitude from critical to supportive. Since my inclination was to see all that was wrong with his ideas, instead of pointing out all that was wrong in the beginning, I sought to use my practicality to help him map out the plan and avoid the pitfalls. God gave me to him to complement his dreams and personality—to help him, not tear him down. When I could foresee a problem, instead of criticizing the dream, I jumped and corrected the issue, or planned around it. I learned to facilitate the dreams he would envision.

Later on, after we had gone through several painful experiences, and once God was given the control in my life to excavate all of the strongholds and hindrances, I was then free to begin to dream again. At that point, it had been so long since I had felt free to dream, that it was very hard for me to allow myself to do so. I knew once I began to think about the

Casey Graves

future and its possibilities, that it would seem scary. To be
loosened from the hold of fear in my life, and then turn
around to commit to doing things that appeared impossible, or
beyond my capabilities, seemed counterintuitive to me.

Even though God had done so much in my life, I still
craved safety. The safety that came with dreaming small,
manageable dreams. But deep inside, I wasn't satisfied with
my own ability, with normal, or with average. I was ready to
see God unleash his gifts into my life, beyond my abilities.
Isn't that what dreaming is? Dreaming is looking past our
own limitations, to reach for what we can't see and what God
can do in our lives. It is longing to see God genuinely change
lives, set people free, and make a real impact on this world
while allowing Him to use us in the process.

That is also the essence of faith. Faith is the confidence
that what we really hope for will actually happen, and gives
us the assurance about things we cannot see (Hebrews 11:1
NLT). Dreaming takes faith, and faith takes dreaming.

For some, dreaming is an idle way to zone out and think
of a far off notion that they will never come to pass. For
others, it is scary and threatens their sense of security. Even
still, others, like my husband, passionately run after
impossibilities and never look back.

Wherever you fit in that spectrum, open your heart up
and dream. Ask God what plans He dreams over your life.
Then know that whatever God places in your heart to strive
for, it is likely to seem impossible. God may not have given
you the ability to accomplish the whole big task all at once,
but every talent, desire and gift you have does give you the
ability to take the small steps you need to begin.

As you begin to dream take it step-by-step and start with
something you *can* do. We can offer God what we *do* have

(which is often completely inadequate) and watch God do miracles with it. As we take each tiny step in the direction of our dream, God turns it into something bigger. Just like the story in Matthew chapter 14, about the boy who gave his lunch. His offering of five loaves of bread and two fish was completely inadequate to do what Jesus needed—to feed five thousand people. But he was *willing* to offer the Savior what he had, and watch Him turn it into a miracle.

Often when God asks me to step out into obedience I feel like what I have to offer is too weak, too small and insignificant. Honestly, I feel like I can't do it. Whatever "it" is. I have to live by the phrase "do it afraid." Most of the things I step out in faith to do, I am doing it—at least at first—afraid. As I have mentioned, I often wonder and ask God why he would choose me to fulfill all these tasks because I'm so keenly aware that I cannot accomplish these tasks on my own.

But that's exactly what God needs from us—He needs us to know that we can't accomplish anything without Him. He is the source of the dream, and equips us to accomplish it. He just needs willing people to take small steps in obedience.

When we take over God's dream for our lives and think we are supremely gifted, talented, or have it all figured out, that's when we operate in our own strength and fail. It's when we realize that anything at all that's good in us, any gift or talent we have, is only from the goodness and graciousness of God, then God can use our lives as an offering to do big things to bring glory to Him.

It is often assumed that dreaming is only for the adventurous and spontaneous. There are certain types of personalities that are labeled as the dreamer type, but everyone has purpose from God to run after. I learned that in the earlier example of using my gifts to facilitate and complement Justin's dreaming with my planning, because accomplishing a dream does take a very practical approach at times. Examining the book of Nehemiah gives us such a great example of someone who heard God's dream, and then laid out a practical, step-by-step approach to accomplish an overwhelming task. Nehemiah was willing, but also humble, and knew he could not realize his dream without God's help.

God birthed a dream in Nehemiah to restore the city walls in Jerusalem and rehabilitate God's people. Nehemiah was in a safe palace in Persia with a comfortable job as the King's cupbearer. He had a visitor report to him of the reprehensible conditions the Jews were experiencing as they returned from captivity back to Jerusalem. When Nehemiah heard this, his immediate reaction was to weep, mourn, fast and pray.

Now that's a response. I can't remember a time that I reacted to news like that about our world and God's people. I hear stories of kidnappings, human trafficking, and hungry, hurting people, yet I have never sat down and wept, mourned, fasted and prayed for days on end about these horrendous circumstances. Nehemiah was receiving a call, a God-sized dream to fulfill. We get to see in Scripture how Nehemiah built that dream.

Nehemiah had an enormous calling to execute, but he began by taking one step at a time. Many times people don't act on their passions for God because they think they cannot make a difference. We feel too small to matter. But if we follow Nehemiah's example, we can see how if we take one obedient step at a time, God can use that to do great things. It doesn't happen overnight, it happens through our faithfulness and consistency of walking out our calling.

## Perfectly Weak

Upon hearing the people of God were in trouble, the first thing Nehemiah did was break down and weep. His first reaction was his heart breaking for the children of God—his heart was aligned with God's heart for God's people. Immediately following that, he began to pray and ask for help and favor from God to begin this God-sized task. He even particularly asked for the King to be favorable and kind to him as he began the project.

Nehemiah modeled great humility. He began in prayer, asking God to forgive him personally, along with his family and his people. He recognized the only chance he has was for God to grant him success. Once God initiated this dream in Nehemiah's heart, and his heart was stirred and broken, he began to plan. Reading through this book, I can picture him as he's fasting, mourning, weeping for days, just pouring over plans in his mind. I can picture him—with his gifts of administration thinking critically and intelligently about how to begin this project. His mind must've been racing and thinking of whom he needed, where to go, and how to start.

All of his planning happens so quickly in the first few chapters. What we can glean from this for our lives is how he gets the news that God's people are in trouble, and he immediately steps into action. He doesn't sit and wonder who else can help them. He didn't think the job was too big, or set that aside for someone else to do. We hear troubling news every day, and see need all around and often think someone else will help in those situations. We have a tendency to become numb to tragedies and pain in our world. It's everywhere, it's rampant and overwhelming. We tend to look the other way.

Nehemiah didn't get overwhelmed and leave the job for someone else to do. He was given the dream from God, and jumped right in. We need to go for it when God breaks our hearts as well. We need to make sure we are allowing God to break our hearts for what breaks His heart.

Nehemiah then begins his journey to inspect the ruins of the city and solidify a plan. He was very wise and deliberate as he made this trip. He didn't tell others and ask their opinions. He surveyed the damage, and calculated the risk and effort it would take. By the time we get to this point walking out our own dreams, we tend to get overwhelmed. If a situation close to our lives is completely destroyed, we tend to fall into despair, doubt, and have the "what am I going to do" attitude. We tend to cower and feel abandoned by God, and not immediately pray and ask God how to restore and rebuild.

Even after Nehemiah saw with his eyes the complete annihilation and destruction Jerusalem had experienced, his immediate response was to rebuild. He was there on a mission. He was not deterred by what he saw, or even what he felt. It doesn't say what he felt in this part of the scripture, but I can imagine while he rode up on the donkey, in the dark, with no one knowing what he was planning yet, with no funding, and no backing from the Jewish officials, that he felt pretty alone. Pretty insignificant. Pretty inadequate. And in those moments, he chose to rebuild. He chose dream of accomplishing something for God and to have confidence in God.

His confidence in God was so strong that he was then able to face opposition. Opposition will come when you step out into building God's dream in your own life. It will come from people you expect it to come from—enemies of God and contentious people—and it will come from people you least expect it—family, friends, coworkers, and fellow servants in the dream with you. When it comes, we can choose to respond like Nehemiah. He said, "The God of Heaven will help us succeed." He knew that promise that, "if God is for you, then who could be against you," before it was even written. Nehemiah was convinced God was with him and confident God would see him through.

As we leave our comfort zone and pursue our God-given dreams, opposition and criticism will come. Nehemiah faced an undercurrent of this throughout the entirety of rebuilding the walls of Jerusalem. His troubles escalated into threats, rage, and plots against him. They began to mock Nehemiah and his efforts, and belittle what he was trying to do. When that comes against you, it makes you question if you're doing the right thing, and if the work you've put in will hold up. Nehemiah is an example of having a laser focus on what God has told him to do, and then blocking out all of the rest.

There have been times that I haven't blocked out all the criticism. I have allowed others' words into my mind and my heart, and have allowed opinions to deter me from the plans God had given me. Listening to the critics can cause discouragement and derailment of the dream. I have actually allowed negative people to change my course and get me off track. Instead of listening to God, I have fallen into the trap of listening to people in attempt to please them.

We've got to tune out all the competition, the opinions, jealousy, negativity, and focus on the One who gave you the dream, the One who opens the doors, and the One who gives you the strength to accomplish the dream. Nehemiah did this, and he responded to this criticism and anger by praying, and working even harder with greater determination in the face of opposition.

In Nehemiah chapter four, Nehemiah prayed in the

difficult times, and told God about the mockers. We can do that, too. Instead of getting even, or giving up, we can just tell God. He knows anyway. He knows what opposition you face now and what you will face in the future. He's taken that into account in the plan He has for you. He will guide you through it and will be your help.

As Nehemiah pushed on and ignored the critics that made them even more furious. The mean people don't go away just because you have a Godly attitude. In fact, sometimes that makes them even more determined to take you out. And as they got more determined to stop Nehemiah, he prayed all the more and worked with continued determination himself.

He put action behind his prayers. Nehemiah didn't just pray to God for help, but he put a plan into action to guard the city from the critics, who had turned vigilantes. It says that they guarded the city night and day from attacks. When you do God's work, there are plans and attacks against you round the clock. You must stay alert, praying and working, as Nehemiah shows us here. To accomplish what God asks us to, we have to learn to push past the critics and discouragement. The two scriptures that illustrate Nehemiah's resolve to keep up God's work are:

Nehemiah 6:3 (NLT) "I am engaged in a great work, so I can't come. Why should I stop working and meet with you?"

Nehemiah 6:9 (NLT) "They were just trying to intimidate us, imagining that they could discourage us and stop the work. So I continued to work with even greater determination."

# Perfectly Weak

When you go after your dream, you are engaged in the great work of God. You have to determine what God says to do and go after it with all your heart. You are pursuing a dream and cannot be disillusioned by the resistance. We can continue our work with even greater determination in the face of intimidation.

And then after all of the distractions, attacks, and all the very hard work through it all, Nehemiah gave God the credit. When you are determined and put the work in, people will realize the work has been done with the help of God.

Nehemiah 6:16 (NLT) "They realized that this work had been done with the help of our God."

I've already shared how overwhelmed and fearfully I responded when God asked me to dream and build Foundations Church. I went through about three years of unbelief and hiding. I didn't immediately respond in determination like Nehemiah. I had to begin to believe and know that just because I felt like I couldn't do something, that didn't disqualify me from it. In fact, that is the very reason God can do something in us. When we can't, God most certainly can.

Believe that you can accomplish big things for God. He calls us to dream in spite of our weaknesses. We are all gifted differently. You are in ministry whether you are an outspoken Elijah—confrontational on the mountaintop—or you are a quiet, yet very faithful stay-at-home mom like Mary, the mother of Jesus, caring for your family. As fellow dreamers, we can't put down one calling or dream for another, and can't diminish your own calling compared to another's. God uses us all according to our gifting's and according to His purposes to impact this world. He put you with a family, a church, a work setting, a friendship that involves a specific dream that only you can fulfill to change the world around you.

Just start. Recognize the dream, and then do the task he puts in front of you. Nehemiah didn't immediately head into Jerusalem big and powerful demanding the wall be rebuilt. He prayed, he asked for favor, he inspected in the dark on a wobbly donkey. For myself, I couldn't start a church. I just couldn't. But I could make crafts with preschoolers. I could write children's ministry policy and procedure manuals. I could organize workers to volunteer. I could unpack tubs every Sunday morning and pack it back up. That was the start. *I realized that as I made myself smaller, with the goal of making God bigger in this world, that God could do anything through me.* I wanted to dream for the purposes of staying so small that God could shine brighter than me. Dream. Then take the steps, and watch God do the miracles.

Chapter Thirteen

# It Takes Discipline

*Exercise daily in God—so no spiritual flabbiness,*
*please! Workouts in the gym are useful, but a disciplined life*
*in God is for more so, making fit both today and forever.*
*1 Timothy 4:8 MSG*

Pray. Read. Exercise. Go to church. Study. Work. Teach
your kids. Consistency. It all takes discipline. And discipline
is carried out when you:
Do it anyway.
Do it if you don't feel like it.
Do it if you're afraid.
Do it if you don't think you have the time.
Do the right thing—over and over again.
Self-help books say that discipline is developing a habit
and then the habit does the job of discipline for you. Some
others say discipline is the ability to know what you should
do, and then do it, whether you feel like it or not. No matter
the definition, discipline is often a lost art in our culture
today. People have lost the concept of delayed gratification,
hard work paying off later, or doing something that doesn't

feel fun, to get the results they want. Instead, people tend to focus on instant gratification, and think hard work is too hard.

In Miriam-Webster's dictionary, discipline means, "training that corrects, molds, or perfects the mental faculties or moral character, orderly or prescribed conduct or pattern of behavior, and self-control."

This is Webster's definition, but you can see Godly implications in this worldly definition. When we are developing discipline, we are in training. We are being corrected, molded, and perfecting mental faculties or moral character. We can frequently see in many around us (and also see in ourselves) the lack of discipline and need for training, correction, and molding. I desperately needed that as a youth pastor's wife heading into church planting. And I will continue to need it as I keep going on my journey. Developing discipline is not a one-time event, but rather a lifelong commitment of hard work that leads you away from self-interest toward an inner dedication to bring Him glory.

The Bible says in Proverbs 5:23 (NIV), "For lack of discipline they will die, led astray by their own great folly." Discipline often gets a bad rap of being boring, predictable and no fun. While it may be all of those things at times, it is also a great source of strength and power in our lives. Proverbs says if we fail to have discipline, we will be led astray. There is great gain in developing discipline and going after what God asks us to with wisdom and obedience. That kind of commitment to discipline benefits all areas of our lives.

The latter part of that definition of discipline prescribes orderly conduct or a pattern of behavior. That, again, is a worldly definition, with Biblical application because our prescribed pattern of behavior and conduct comes from the

Bible. We must have discipline to actually read the Bible, and not just read and study it, but to read and apply it to our lives. When we are disciplined to activate God's Word in our lives that leads to discipline in other areas of our lives as well.

To receive the blessing of direction and God-sized results in our lives, we must cultivate discipline and develop the Godly habits that we need. If we don't have the discipline to read God's Word and actually apply it to our lives, we are like the man looking in a mirror that forgets what he looks like. James 1:22-25 (NIV) "Do not merely listen to the word, and so deceive yourselves. Do what it says. Anyone who listens to the word but does not do what it says is like someone who looks at his face in a mirror and, after looking at himself, goes away and immediately forgets what he looks like. But whoever looks intently into the perfect law that gives freedom, and continues in it—not forgetting what they have heard, but doing it—they will be blessed in what they do."

Self-control is also one of the descriptors of discipline. When we are spiritually disciplined, the Holy Spirit is given the access to our lives to develop the fruit of the Spirit in us. This enables us to operate bearing fruit in our daily lives. Being fruitful sounds like a very elementary Sunday School principle, but it's not as easy as it sounds. Having a posture of love, joy, and peace alone is against every ounce of our human nature at times. Self-control cannot be attained just by trying. That is evident when we try walking in love when someone hurts your child. Or we attempt to be patient when someone is yelling at us or personally attacking. Try having gentleness and self-control when your older child sneaks out and lies to your face. Try finding peace when you get a diagnosis of cancer. The fruit of the Spirit is produced in us as we consistently seek after God and allow Him to bring the change we need.

For example, while I was a stay-at-home-mom while both of my children were under the age of five, I came to grips with the "ugly" side of mommy-ing. I found myself, more often than not, losing my temper, yelling, and rushing my children impatiently. Many times, there was no joy or peace. While some of that is normal, and might sound like a very common description of that stage of parenting, it really grieved me that I was out of control at times. I learned that as I would yell and throw a fit, I would then see that behavior again later on in the day from my toddlers throwing it right back at me.

I was tired. I was with tiny humans all day every day. I was overwhelmed. And I was not operating in the fruit of the Spirit. As I recognized that about myself, I began a journey to grow as a person in discipline and self-control. Instead of trying to figure out how to control the children better, I realized I needed discipline in my own life to control myself.

I acknowledged that operating in the fruit of the Spirit in this stage was not something I could do on my own. I needed the Holy Spirit to produce that in me. I needed the discipline to come to Him daily and seek help from God and His Word, and refocus on Him.

Being fruitful isn't just shown in what we accomplish for others to see. It is, many times, found in things that we don't do. It's when we choose to act in patience and love, instead of reacting in anger. We are fruitful when we can operate in joy even when our circumstances are less than joyful. We can't function like that without with the Holy Spirit's help and without a life of disciplined thoughts wrought from Bible study, prayer, and seeking God. We can only be disciplined while setting our minds under the control of the Holy Spirit.

"The mind controlled by the Spirit brings life and peace," is a scripture I really do quote every day. I have to make a conscious effort to yield my mind to the Holy Spirit every day. That goes along with 2 Timothy that said God gives us a spirit of self-discipline. We have to choose to operate in that self-discipline. It takes choosing every day to wake up and say, "God I give you mind, my thoughts, my words, and I choose to let my mind be Spirit-controlled." That is the beginning of discipline.

In fact, the entire chapter of Romans 8 is amazing, and guides us on having disciplined thought-life. Romans 8:5-8 says, "Those who live according to the sinful nature have their minds set on what that nature desires; but those who live in accordance with the Spirit have their minds set on what the Spirit desires. The mind of the sinful man is death, but the mind controlled by the Spirit brings life and peace; the sinful mind is hostile to God. It does not submit to God's law, nor can it do so. Those controlled by the sinful nature cannot please God."

That's a whole bunch of saying that we need to be disciplined.

We can't be controlled by our own desires, our own natures. We can't give into what our flesh wants. We can't do what the rest of the world around us is doing. The only thing that brings life is having our mindset controlled by the Spirit. It says in verse 5 that our minds are going to be set on something. It's either set on what our sinful nature desires, or it's set on what the Spirit desires. If we get a choice (which we do), we might as well set it in the direction of God's blessing, life and peace.

If we choose to develop discipline and relinquish control of our mind to the Spirit, verse 11 reveals that the same Spirit that you are allowing to control your mind raised Christ from the dead and is living in you. I want that kind of power allowed to guide my life. That is the kind of power that is strong in our weakness and can empower to change this world and live out God-sized dreams.

So, we choose discipline to allow God to produce fruitfulness in our lives, not just for our own change, but to impact this world with God's life changing power. Training is preparation by God to accomplish His will in us. We use discipline to study His Word to tune into God's voice so we can be attentive enough to God to hear Him when He speaks to us. We want to be ready when He's ready to use us.

When promotion or increase comes, and God says it's time to step up, our commitment level to discipline will show if we are prepared. You prepare, train, and practice because you want to be prepared to run toward what God calls you to, not run away from it (as I did initially when we planted the church). You want to be sure and confident in God's ability in you, not shrink back in fear. Training is activity to commit to in order to develop skilled behavior. If you're disciplined, day in and day out, you'll be prepared, skilled ready when God sends the advance.

That type of day-in-day-out preparation makes me think of habitual routine, like when I played basketball. I was a pretty good basketball player, but I wasn't great because of my mind and low confidence level. I went to a small school in Texas, so I was able to play most sports that I wanted to. I was very athletic and loved sports. I practiced a lot and was very disciplined at pushing myself. My dad played sports with me every chance he got, and helped me train.

# Perfectly Weak

I can remember practicing often, and I don't remember hating it—but actually liking it. I remember being age seven, and moving from tee-ball to coach pitch softball. Every night in our yard, my dad would pitch soft balls to me to practice hitting until it was dark. He would make me hit ten in a row before we could go in. That's discipline. I remember when I got serious about basketball my dad got the measurements of the basketball court and painted the three-point line, the foul shot line and the court onto our circle drive way where my basketball hoop was. I practiced into the evening many nights. That's repetitive training and its discipline. I practiced when the gym was open in the summer, I played summer league, I went to camps, and I went to two-a-days.

That is all a very simplistic example of developing discipline, not spiritual discipline, but easily relatable to different experiences in our lives. However, through all of that practicing, I did not work on my mind, or my confidence level. I didn't really know I could back then. Even in high school I could've come to God's Word. I could've learned to focus better, and disciplined with my thoughts. I could shoot, pass, dribble, but there were times I was so hesitant in games that I didn't want the ball. I knew I could play, but I wasn't confident. I let my feelings reign over my ability. In clutch moments, I didn't want the ball.

In our God-sized dream, we need to want the ball. We, as Christ followers, need to be ready for the dream when God calls us and sends the promotion. We need the desire to jump out there when God says to. Lack of self-discipline can cause us to be timid and shy away from opportunities that God brings, or miss hearing His voice. Having a consistent routine with God—including Him in your everyday life makes us ready and prepared for the next step.

Many times we neglect to develop discipline in our spiritual lives because we are so busy "doing." We get overwhelmed and caught in our schedules, and in the details of our lives. We are busy at our places of employment, with our families and children, extracurricular activities, and daily routines. Those are all added things into our lives. We need to remember that we aren't here on Earth to do all those things. We are here for God and for His purposes. He reminds us in Matthew 6:33 to seek Him first and then *all these things* will be added to you.

With busy schedules and mile long to-do lists, many times we forget to seek Him first. I have family, people, projects, ministries that I needed added into my life, and it's hard not to focus on them solely. I have to remind myself that I must start with seeking Him. I have to put Him first, and then its God job to add all the details into my life and accomplish His purpose in me. I must diligently focus on God and His Kingdom and not get wrapped up in my own kingdom. I choose to let go of all the *things* and take hold of Him.

John chapter 15:4-5 (NIV), "Remain in Me, and I will remain in you. No branch can bear fruit by itself; it must remain in the vine. Neither can you bear fruit unless you remain in Me. I am the vine; you are the branches. If a man remains in Me and I in him, he will bear much fruit; apart from Me you can do nothing." I have learned that I cannot stay disciplined and bear fruit without God's help. I can't do all those things that I want added into my life—accomplish all the tasks and details that I am so busy with—without God. That is so ironic, because we usually neglect spiritual discipline because we are busy doing all the things we can't do on our own anyway. If we would focus and seek God first, He will enable us to do what we need.

It's only through disciplined preparation, doing the right thing day in and day out, even when others never see, you are sure and confident in what God has done in you and what He can do through you. You don't get there by will power. You get there by daily going to God and yielding your thoughts for His thoughts, exchanging your control for His control, and being disciplined to let God prepare you. That kind of preparation is done in the quiet moments when no one else is around. Mark Batterson refers to this as "repeated obedience" in his book "The Grave Robber." And repeated obedience—doing the right thing God has asked of you, over and over and over definitely takes discipline—especially when no one is looking.

When you bypass that kind of discipline, that preparation from God, then you have second-guessing, and doubt. If you're practiced enough in a sport, you don't have to think about it to run or dribble. You get those automatic responses from repetitive training. If you've practiced, then its second nature.

Doing the right thing, the disciplined thing over and over again, yields a result of being ready for God to catapult you into action. If you've been disciplined to spend time in God's presence, you *know* His Voice; have been prepared in season and out of season. You'll have an automatic response to God when He says to move, to talk to that person, to pray for someone, to step out in faith. Discipline in God's Word allows God to replace your old nature, with your new nature in Christ Jesus.

Moses was prepared in the desert alone. Joseph was prepared in the dungeon alone. It may take longer than you want—and it probably will—and take you places out of the way, and you may seem forgotten, but God still sees you. You're being developed by the Almighty God your Father who knows you best and where you need to be. Be disciplined enough to continue when it's long, or boring, or lonely, or hard. Discipline isn't popular, or fun, or recognized by anyone, but it yields God-sized results.

So don't rush through it. Don't take the easy way out. Make the extra effort and go the long way around. Climb the hill with God and see what He can do.

Chapter Fourteen

# It Takes Letting Go

Most people struggle with control. It's very cliché to say that we have "control issues" these days. But it's often said because it's true. In regards to our purpose and pursuits in life, we have to let go of control to allow God to bring about His dream in our life the way He wants it, in His timing, in the place He wants. The one thing I have seen in my life, and learned, is that God is always surprising. I have heard the scripture, in Isaiah chapter 55, over and over that says, "God's ways are higher than our ways and His thoughts are higher than our thoughts." And yes, I sometimes get tired of hearing that because I am stuck with my own thoughts that can't always understand the infinite God of the universe. I wish I had God's thoughts. I wish I knew what He was thinking. I wish I knew why at times. But I don't. There are circumstances and situations that happen we just can't understand.

God does things contrary to our understanding because He's bigger than us. He's bigger than our world and He sees all the way to the end. He holds the big picture in His hands. The good news is that He's in this with us for our best interest, and for His Glory. He loves us more than we could ever even imagine and He can do above and beyond all we could ask or imagine with our lives. But it hardly ever looks like we think it will look.

If I want to get from point A to point B, or from step one to step two, I would want to walk in the straightest, fastest route there. I am a rusher. I like to do things fast, check them off my list, and call it done. But almost always God will wind me through what seems like a crazy maze—sometimes even going in circles similarly to the Israelites—to finally arrive at point B. It could've been straight there, could've been faster, or easier. That would've made sense, but that's not the way it always works.

Along the curvy maze path, we learn and grow, and we become less of self and more of Him. We begin to give Him our weaknesses and operate in His strength to find that His grace is sufficient. It's along the way we seek Him wholeheartedly because we are at the end of our rope. And then it happens, *we give up control.*

It's an amazing feeling to finally give up and let God just do what He wants. The truth is, He is doing what He wants anyway. He's just waiting for you and I to let go of all the controlling, stressed worrying, and grumbling to enjoy what He's doing. The first couple years we started the church, I hid because I couldn't handle the worry of how it was all going to happen, and how people would treat us. I tried to figure it all out, instead of believing and trusting. **Once I finally let it all go, I realized I don't have to handle any of it. God handles it for me.** You've got to realize that If God calls you to the dream, He handles it. We are literally just conduits for His calling.

It's His dream. It's His purpose for His Kingdom. If it's all His, He does the work. He handles the pressure. He provides. He does it all through us if we let Him. If He is doing it all anyway, we can choose to relax and enjoy it. We can sit back and watch. When we truly learn to sit back and watch, it's freeing. It's peaceful to know God's responsible for it all to work out.

This type of freedom and peace happens when you are:

-listening to hear the dream and know its God's calling for you

-stepping out to take the risk for Him

-putting in the hard work and effort to *do* for God and then also *be* with God to have

-overcoming the strongholds in your life and begin walking in power

-trusting Him

-staying humble

-keeping your motives pure

-being disciplined

Then you are doing all you can do. When you are doing your part in obedience, then you get to sit back and watch God move. That, I will tell you, is so fun. God's part is fun to watch. You can watch him change situations that you could never change. You can watch Him provide people in your path, resources, or finances that you never in your wildest dreams could come up with. You can watch Him do for you that which you cannot do for yourself. He does this because you are His child, because He loves you, and He is furthering His Kingdom through you.

Two of my favorite quotes about letting God have control are, "You obey God and let God handle the consequences," and, "When you feel all you have left is God, and only He can help, that's the best place to be." Sometimes God takes us to places where we have to be totally reliant upon Him to proceed or even survive, and that is when He works best. He is faithful and His promises are sure to come through for you. One of my husband's favorite versions of the beatitudes is out of the Message translation. It says, "You are blessed when you are at the end of your rope, for that's when with less of you there's more of Him, and His rule."

Another Scripture I have really focused on when learning to let go of control is Psalm 119:105 (NIV) and says, "Your word is a lamp for my feet, a light on my path." As my husband and I were youth pastors, he preached a lot about finding and following God's will for your life. Teenagers and college-aged people are right in the throes of navigating that scary process.

My husband used to preach from this scripture as guidance. He gave such an amazing illustration that the Holy Spirit has now brought back around to my life about letting go of control, and letting go of the "not knowing" how things will work out. It's really difficult to step out into the dream God gives you without knowing all of the steps in advance. You don't know where to go next, or how it's going to end.

This scripture tells us that God's Word is a lamp unto our feet. A lamp. Not a floodlight. God isn't telling us here He's going to show us the entire plan. He's not saying that He will show us the twenty-year spreadsheet prospectus. He is saying He will show you where to put your foot next.

If you are walking in the dark with a lamp, you can really only see your next few steps ahead. When I am lying in bed with only the lamp on, I can't even see into the bathroom. I can't see outside. I can't see down the hall or around the corner. By using the type of small lantern likely written about in this psalm, you really only could see what was right in front of you. We are meant to only see what is right in front of us.

Let go of what is down the road. Let go of trying to see farther than you're supposed to, wanting to know what's next, and see what is right in front of you to do. Take the next step He is showing you without having to know what's next. And trust that He won't let you stumble. That is what a lamp is used for—to keep you on sure-footing while you're walking in the dark. Trust that once you are obedient in the current step you just took, that He will show you the next one.

Even after God pulled me in the direction of completely letting go and trusting Him, I still had the thoughts of *what if I don't like the next step? What if I can't do the next step?* I had to learn to trust the lamp and let go of having to know, and trust that every moment of my life is orchestrated by God. God even arranges the small things in our lives. When we can see how He sets up the little things, we can trust so much more that He's orchestrating the big. It's just like how He has told us that if He cares enough to see the sparrow and clothe the lily, then how much more will He care for us?

He planned ahead for me, and He goes before you to make a way as well. Tiny things that happen, places you go, people you meet, words you say or are said to you, are all God moments, and we don't even realize it. He's always setting us up. We don't connect the dots until later, or sometimes never. He is always moving, and working, and setting events in motion—mostly while we don't see. That's why it's fun to sit back and watch. Sometimes you get to see the Divine.

When you let go, you get to marvel at the sovereignty of God. The first five years we planted the church, God brought people to us, and did things for us, that we didn't even know we needed or wanted. He went before us and set us up even better than we could have imagined or planned. For example, when we were in the very first moments of figuring out how to move to Tulsa and get started, we couldn't find a house to rent. We had owned three small fixer-upper homes before. We had great credit. No money, no job, but great credit. We had always been able to get a loan and been good stewards with what God provided. But with no job, no solid source of consistent income, after ten years of marriage, we couldn't get a loan. Plus, we were venturing out into a church plant and had no idea what a salary would be, if any, in the next years to come. So, a bank, understandably, was not going to loan us money.

We had to rent a house. I have mentioned how we went about frantically securing the rent house earlier, and we ran into the same situation with the landlord as the bank. They did not want to rent us the house without a co-signer. My parents had to cosign. As I mentioned before, there was only one house in the entire area to rent, and I was annoyed with this. I wanted options. I wanted a good deal. We could just find the one house.

I wasn't even sure if this was the house we wanted, but we had to move fast to get it. Why did this happen so fast? I didn't connect the dots at first. God had ordained it. It was His design for us to not getting a loan. He arranged the fact that we had to rent and this house was the only one open. It was for us because there were people on that street for us to meet. I still didn't connect those dots as we moved in.

The neighborhood was perfect for us. It had a park, a neighborhood pool, and many young families. The very first weekend we were there, we were walking back from the park with the girls in strollers and we heard someone yell, "Justin Graves? Is that you?"

I was definitely taken aback. Honestly, I was still so caught in the raw emotion of the move that I wanted to run. Plus, no one even knew we were there. I almost felt like we were in hiding. We are heading into an impossible, daunting task—which people usually thought we were crazy for attempting—so we were keeping our heads down and not really broadcasting our situation and location. We were deflated, embarrassed, and scared.

So, who knew us in this new place? Well, turns out, we had been youth pastors in Tulsa a few years back. One of the kids in our group, who was now in college, had cousins that lived two doors down from our new rent house. These cousins also had a baby they were taking to the park, right by our new rent house. And these cousins were being accompanied by their aunt, who was the kids' parent that we had youth pastored several years prior.

The aunt recognized Justin. We went over and they introduced us and said, "They just moved here too. They don't know anyone and they need a church." I don't believe that my life is left to chance or coincidence. This was a God ordained meeting right there on the sidewalk. The rest is history, and that history includes some very amazing friends that we made who started the church with us from day one, and are still here —even after a move to Colorado and back. Even better, more of their family has moved into town and is attending Foundations as well. God let no other house be available for rent except that one, to meet those people, on that day. And boy did we need that. And they did too.

The dots started to connect. The very first weekend in town to start this dream adventure, God had ordained. God had gone before, and set us up. Around that time, my eyes and heart started to open and see God moving. I began to watch and marvel at the sovereignty of God. The first ten years of marriage and ministry had left me with so many unanswered prayers, so much teaching others to do what I felt like I couldn't do, and so much disappointment. I had lost the child-like faith in believing that God takes care of every little detail in life because I had seen so many details that I felt were left unattended.

I was starting to realize all over again that God had always been there setting up our lives even when—especially when—I couldn't see it or feel it. God was reminding me that He was in control. God showed me in a real and tangible way that year this scripture, Acts 17:24-28 says, "The God who made the world and everything in it is the Lord of heaven and earth and does not live in temples built by human hands. And He is not served by human hands, as if He needed anything. Rather, He Himself gives everyone life and breath and everything else. From one man He made all the nations, that they should inhabit the whole earth; and He marked out their appointed times in history and the boundaries of their lands. God did this so that they would seek Him and perhaps reach out for Him and find Him, though He is not far from any one of us. For in Him we live and move and have our being."

These verses met me at a time when I needed to be reminded that He gave me life and breath, and put me here on earth at this time in history in the exact city and neighborhood in which He needed me to reside. The magnitude of all that hit me really hard. God wasn't about to abandon me because He put me here for this exact moment and place in time to do something for Him, to build His Kingdom.

# Perfectly Weak

God continued to show up in miraculous ways for us in this launching phase, proving over and over He had been working all along in our lives. When we moved into the rent house, we had a friend that had built a house just right around the corner from our neighborhood that he needed to sell. A lady had the house built, and then backed out of the contract. The house had been sitting, waiting for a buyer for a while. This was right around the time of the big housing bust and economic downfall in the early 2000's.

Our friend approached us about purchasing the house, and we told him that we were renting and couldn't buy at the time. He wanted Justin to see the house. So Justin went to see it and immediately said exactly these words, "Oh man, there's no way we could ever afford this house. No way." So we continued to rent our house for a year.

Nearing the end of the year rental contract, we started looking around to buy a house. Justin had the idea to call this friend up and see if the house was still sitting and available. I, being the not-so-optimistic-person at times, thought it was a waste of time because it was completely out of the question and out of our price range. It was beyond our capacity. Not even close.

But Justin still went to see the house and talk to the guy. And after the year was up, the house was still sitting, waiting on a buyer. Justin told him that the house was way out of our price range. They ended the conversation with the friend asking him how much we could afford, which was lower than what it cost to build the house. Justin came home and told me that the guy said, "I will see what we can do."

So my reaction to that was to continue to look around at other affordable options. And Justin kept his mind open, while mine was closed to that particular house. I was looking at what I could do. He was looking at what God could do. Pretty quickly, our friend called us with this news that the owner of the company decided that we could purchase the house for what Justin told him we could afford.

They took a loss on the house. So that means that God had that house built a couple years before we even moved back to Tulsa. He had it sitting there. Just waiting on us. We didn't ask for this house when we moved to plant the church. We didn't expect it. We didn't even know we wanted it. God brings things you don't even know you want sometimes, because He knows more than we do. It's fun to sit back and watch God move on your behalf.

Another example of God's provision for us was finding a meeting location for our church. As soon as we moved to Tulsa, we began searching out a place for Foundations Church to meet on Sundays. We didn't have a church building, so we looked at movie theaters, grocery stores and schools. We had this particular school district in mind that we just knew was where God wanted us. We tried every way possible to get them to work with us, and there was no budging. Justin was pretty frustrated with this process as we couldn't find the right fit. We were less than thrilled with the venue in which we secured to finally launch the church. It was a terrible location that with poor visibility.

It was hidden, and old. And a little stinky and dirty. The nursery babies were playing in a locker room, and the older children met in a high school band room. I swept the band rooms frequently on Sunday mornings and picked up paper clips, hairballs, dust balls, tacks, old band aids, pennies...not the perfect place for toddlers to crawl around. I told Justin several times that I couldn't believe people with small children would come to our church. I even told him that I probably wouldn't come just because of the kids' facilities. In fact, Chloe, who was eighteen months old when we started the church, came out of the locker room/nursery every week and her feet were black because they were so dirty from that floor. I couldn't even think about how gross that was. I just had to overlook it.

I say all of that to point out that we totally thought we were disadvantaged. We didn't connect the dots. We didn't think this was God-orchestrated, until we had been there three years and that older couple from the Lutheran church down the street came to visit and offered us their building.

God put us where He wanted us, and then He sent them. We did not like our launching location. We thought it hindered our efforts and wanted to be somewhere else. But the only way we miraculously and out of the blue had a church building land on top of us, is because we were placed in that exact spot, for those church people to see us, and be generous to us. We didn't orchestrate anything. God went before us and set us up. It was ordained by Him. We tried and tried to make it happen any other way. We got to watch God move on our behalf.

If you need people to help you, or contribute in your ministry, you have to know He has already got them ready and waiting for the right time in His Plan. He knows the people you need to meet. In fact, when you happen to bump into a person at Starbucks that can do exactly what you need, and they want to help you, that's God's timing and provision. Sometimes we take those types of events in our lives as chance meetings, or lucky coincidences, but they are God ordained. He sets it up. He's doing it all the time.

If you need financial provision, He owns all the money in the world. There was a time in my life that I found it completely impossible to be able to fix both of our broken transmissions, buy groceries, and pay for hospital bills. I never understood God's timing and why we seemed to always be in need, but I always received what I needed in His timing, in His way. God is always on time. He's got this for you. He's gone ahead to prepare what you need. If you need a house, a church building, childcare, volunteers, favor with city contractors or approval for something, God makes it all happen. He's already working on what you need.

In anticipation, be looking around every corner for His answer. Trust that if you do what you are supposed to do that God will do what you cannot. He has already set in motion events that are supposed to happen in your life. You've got to wait and trust. Remembering that it's His plan and His kingdom that He is furthering through you is key to trusting He will give you what you need—although sometimes in a roundabout way or surprising fashion.

With all of the examples from the first five years of planting and leading this church—and literally dozens more—I cannot wait to see what is going to happen in the next five years. I am literally on the edge of my seat with Holy expectation and anticipation. You need to be there for your life as well. If you are developing God's dream for you, pursuing Him, then expect Him to move. Watch for it. Wake up every day asking for it, looking for it. Be sure to let go of trying to control it and trying to figure it out.

I am the person that once completely gave up hope of anything good happening to me again and now I am transformed by God's goodness, mercy and grace into the person that is waiting to see amazing and miraculously God-orchestrated events around every corner. I am excited. And what's even better, I know He is going to bring things around again that we don't even know we need or want. I know that the next five years of my life will look completely different than I could even imagine.

Along the way I have learned to stop telling God what to do. I've stopped praying for what I want, and instead ask Him what He wants for me, because He always does better than I could at setting up my life. I have continually submitted to His desires, telling God *I want what You want*. Sure, I have things I want God to do, but I yield those desires to the King and ask for His desires over my own.

I have settled into the knowledge that He totally knows better than me what I need. Sometimes we feel completely out of control of how our life is going—especially if we are genuinely and obediently following a God given dream. You feel like you can't see what's coming. Let me tell you, that's the best place in the world to be. He can see what's coming. He has already gone before you in time and set it up. And he knows what is in your heart, because he formed that too. He made you for your town, for the people you live with, for the church you go to, for this ministry you are in, and if you're pursuing Him, He will give you the desires of your heart. See Psalm 37:4. When you connect all these dots, you realize it is out of the realm of our imagination and capacity to understand. We don't get it. But God does. And that's really the best place to be.

CPSIA information can be obtained at www.ICGtesting.com
Printed in the USA
LVOW11s1116180516

488731LV00003B/4/P